THE MAN THEY CALL MR GRAPHOLOGY

Fraser White is recognised as one of the world's foremost graphologists.

He is known as Mr Graphology to millions of radio listeners who have been impressed and sometimes startled by the accuracy of his handwriting analyses of famous personalities.

Under his miscroscope for instance has come the handwriting of the Prime Minister, Harold Wilson . . . and Fraser White's analysis became a national talking point.

Regularly featured on the Pete Murray record request radio programme Open House and at times on other radio and TV programmes in Britain and overseas, Fraser White now receives more than 400 letters every week.

WHAT THE CELEBRITIES SAY ABOUT MR GRAPHOLOGY . . .

WENDY CRAIG—"I am amazed how he can read all this from my handwriting—it is all very true."

VAL DOONICAN—"I think it's marvellous and absolutely fascinating."

JON PERTWEE—"This man is a genius."

HARRY SECOMBE—"I'm going red here."

CILLA BLACK—"He's good is Fraser White . . . he's smashing!"

VIOLET CARSON—"Fraser White is astonishingly right. He's good."

Handwriting Secrets

Fraser White

EVEREST BOOKS LIMITED
4 Valentine Place, London SE1 01-261 1536

Published in Great Britain by Everest Books Ltd 1974

ISBN: 0 903925 052

Made and printed in Great Britain by
Hunt Barnard Printing Ltd., Aylesbury, Bucks

To my father Arthur White,
founder of the White Write System of graphology

MY THANKS . . .

. . . To The British Broadcasting Corporation for helping to inspire national interest in graphology.

. . . To Mark White, Head of Radio 1 in 1971, who approved executive producer Doreen Davies' idea that graphology be featured on "The Jimmy Young Show".

. . . To Jimmy Young and his producer Paul Williams for transforming an essentially visual subject into good-listening radio.

. . . To Pete Murray who has learned to read my own unruly handwriting when I rush the analyses into his studio—and who stops some of the celebrities coming into the control room to clobber me!

. . . To Ray Harvey, producer of "Open House", and his predecessor Peter Bell.

. . . To Joe Bronkhorst for his kindly personal help to me.

. . . To my father Arthur White, who was the pioneer of graphology in this country.

. . . To the more than 200 guest celebrities I have analysed on the radio.

. . . To the more than 10,000 listeners who have written to me.

. . . And finally to my Personal Assistant, Michael Elmhirst, for his enthusiasm and organising ability that allowed this book to be published.

Fraser White.

Foreword by
PETE MURRAY

Everyone loves a success story. And no one connected with "Open House" is more delighted than I that Fraser White's handwriting analysis has caught the imagination of our vast morning listening audience.

But I'll let you into a secret: when it was first suggested that the show should include a graphology spot every morning, I had misgivings. I just couldn't imagine that reading the character of our guests by their handwriting would have radio appeal. And, what's more, I doubted whether Fraser, much as I like and respect him, could possibly be accurate in his findings.

We all make mistakes!

That dreaded moment, when our famous guests have their intimate personality secrets revealed to eight million listeners, has become one of the highlights of an already popular programme.

From the letters we receive, it is obvious that thousands of listeners will not go out shopping or slip round to a neighbour's for coffee until they have heard what Fraser is about to divulge about their favourite personality.

Why so popular? Simple. Fraser, more often than not, is bang on target with his analysis . . . and he has an uncanny knack of hitting on unique personality traits he could not possibly have gleaned from Press cuttings or from knowing the stars personally. It is not surprising that Fraser's own fan mail has leaped unbelievably since his first analysis was broadcast in my programme in August, 1973. Housewives and business people alike all write in for graphology tips and general handwriting advice.

But, as the programme's host, it's also a little bit worrying for me. You see, they're even writing to Fraser for requests now!

At "Open House" we've naturally had a lot of fun with Fraser's enviable talent. Looking back over the 200 or so shows we've done together, I can remember some hilarious moments when his findings have reduced certain guests to red-faced, speechless embarrassment and wide-eyed disbelief at his accuracy.

Listeners would have been amazed if they could have seen **Virginia Wade** when she was asked to give Fraser a handwriting sample. The tennis star, normally ice-cool and unflappable on court, was shaking. "I'm too scared," she said. Fraser finally persuaded her, but Virginia was in agony until I'd finished reading Fraser's analysis. Then, with a relieved sigh, she said: "Ah, well, that wasn't too bad, was it?"

Jimmy Edwards wasn't so happy, though. After Fraser had described him as "dogmatic", Jimmy turned to me and said: "If I'd known, I'd have brought my horse whip."

However, the bouquets outnumber the brickbats. The best praise came from **Sir Bernard Miles.** After a praiseworthy analysis he said: "The BBC ought to double Fraser's fees."

Actress **Dolores Gray** expressed her thanks with a warm kiss—much to Fraser's delighted surprise!

There were many times, too, when an intimate observation brought funny quips from the "victim".

Remember **Michael Crawford,** for example. I read out Fraser's note that Michael had "coy virility"—and, quick as a flash, Michael came back with: "Does that mean I do it with the lights out?"

I mean to say, some mothers do 'ave 'em, don't they?

Sex, naturally, provides the best ground for good-natured joking and, unknown to the listeners, we all had a giggle after Fraser wrote that Doctor in the House star, **Robin Nedwell** had "an insatiable sexual appetite".

Shortly after I read the Robin Nedwell analysis over the air, a BBC girl had to bring me the latest motoring news. But she refused to go into the studio while Robin was with me . . . "in case her virtue was at stake".

Robin took it all in good part, naturally.

It is these never-publicised quirks that the fans want to know about.

Watching the embarrassed looks of my guests when it's time for Fraser's analysis amuses me a lot. But my own blushing moment came not so long ago when, unknown to me, **Leslie Phillips** had been handed a slip of paper with my own analysis.

Imagine my own embarrassment as I sat there, helpless, listening to him read: "Pete Murray has now reached the age when his sex life is at a simmer. . . . "

What did I say about Fraser White having the knack? About him hitting the nail on the head? I retract that!

Seriously, though, this is a fascinating book and I'm sure you'll enjoy it.

Good luck, Fraser.

CHAPTER ONE

Graphology is no fairground sideshow attraction. It is a serious science based on powers of observation and expert opinion, which has proved to be reliable over years of tests.

It cannot tell if you will marry a tall dark handsome stranger or if you will inherit a fortune.

What it can tell you is:

> Whether you have the ability to mix easily with the opposite sex.
> Whether you have the ability to make a fortune.
> Whether you are an egotist or basically a shy person.
> Whether you have business abilities.
> Whether you have natural artistic capabilities or whether you have a "show business" flair.
> Whether or not you can be trusted with a confidence.
> Whether you are resigned to being a natural loser or have the determination to succeed.
> Whether sexually you are an introvert or an extrovert.

The quality of handwriting reveals brain-power and concentration.

It is a curious fact there is a simile on matters of copying between the copper-plate writers of the Victorian era and rock 'n' roll fans of the Fifties.

In the Victorian era they slavishly and mindlessly followed the writing examples of their "superiors"—their parents or their bosses.

In the rock 'n' roll era they slavishly and mindlessly followed the styles, writing and otherwise, of their "superiors"—this time pop idols.

Every day I meet people who say: "You can never analyse my handwriting because it changes every time I write."

The truth is your handwriting does not change basically. The changes are superficial according to your moods.

If you doubt this, have a look at specimens of your handwriting as done on different days.

Check on the circumstances and the mood you were in at the time of writing. Were you feeling happy, mellow or depressed?

Now look at the formation of your written letters. Where are the t crosses placed? Do your letters a and o keep open or closed? Does the placing of the i dots over the stems of each letter change? Do the loops in your letters g and y look different? Do you find that your letters within the words are connected or are they disjointed?

You will find that most of these vital points of the character analysis are consistently similar.

The slope of your lines of the handwriting may change; the slant of the handwriting may change; the size of your handwriting may change . . . but that is according to your mood of the moment. Your writing can have its own happy or disgruntled look, yet the basic style is unchanged.

If you compare the variations of your handwriting against the features that dominate the specimens, you will find major clues to your natural character.

Try this and compare it with the guide I give you later in the book. Then you will begin to realise the accuracy of graphology.

The basic principle of an accurate graphological analysis is that the sample should be written naturally by a person in average mood.

However, even if a person deliberately tries to disguise his or her handwriting, clues to basic character of the person will still be apparent to an experienced graphologist.

The purpose of this book is to provide a guide to handwriting analysis in a manner that will give you valuable clues from every form of writing. All letters will become a source of fascination. For young people some knowledge of graphology could provide a new awareness in the powers of observation and may even help to show the way to a new career.

CHAPTER TWO

Like a face, handwriting can reveal the mood of the owner. Minor changes may take place but clues to the basic character of the person remains unchanged.

For an example, look at these two specimens of handwriting (Figures 1 and 2). You might think at a glance these are written by two different people.

In fact, these are specimens written by the same person in different moods.

The writer is Jon Pertwee, known throughout the world as television's "Doctor Who".

When I received the first sample of his handwriting I was not convinced that it was his natural everyday writing.

There were two danger signals: the unusually large size of writing and the horizontal slope of the lines which dropped down to an alarming degree.

This illustrated to me that Jon was under severe emotional strain and in a state of complete physical exhaustion at the time of writing the first sample.

The contents of his second sample confirmed the accuracy of this analysis.

As you see here, he states that at the time of writing the first sample he was indeed under extreme emotional pressure and physically exhausted.

However, this was a temporary condition.

In the second sample Jon's handwriting is still rather larger than average but the horizontal level of the lines has lifted and now goes in a straight rightward direction across the page.

Apart from these two variations all other characteristics in the two samples are identical.

The graphological pointers illustrate that Jon is full of animation and nervous energy and that mentally he is a live-wire.

The shape of the letters confirms he has a restless nature and that he has a tendency to have a rather quick temper.

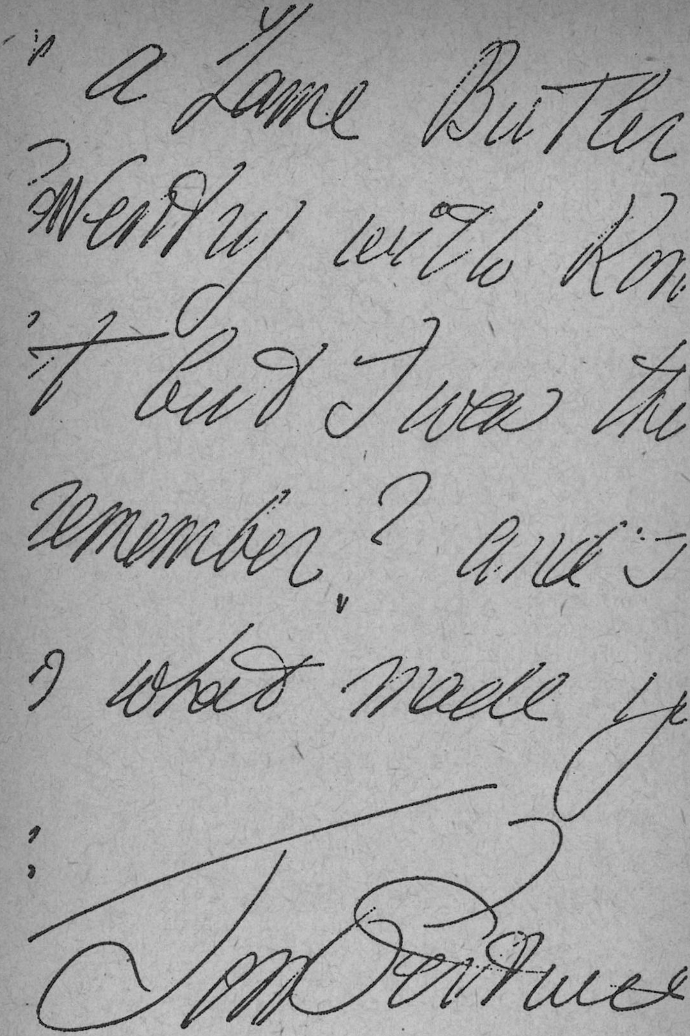

FIGURE 1

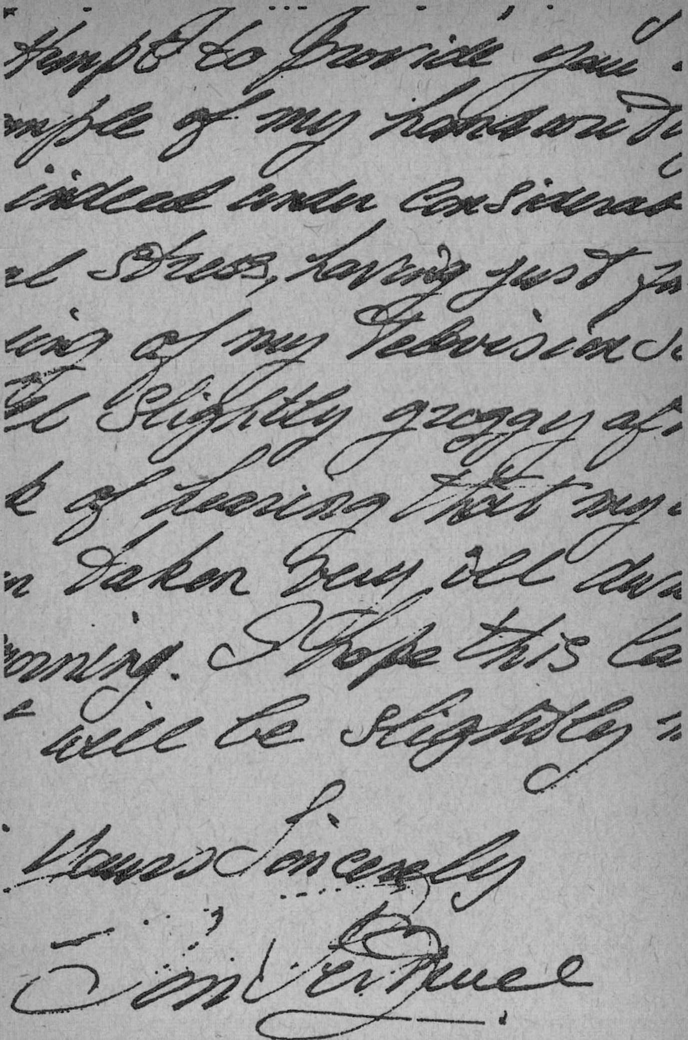

...tempt to provide you...
...mple of my handwriti...
...indeed under considera...
...al stress, having just ...
...ing of my television s...
...still slightly groggy af...
...k of hearing that my ...
...n taken very ill dur...
...orning. I hope this la...
...will be slightly ...

Yours Sincerely

...

FIGURE 2

15

The long final strokes indicate he has a generous and extravagant side to his nature.

Where these finals fly back over the word in a loop, the considerate side of his nature and his desire to protect himself and others is illustrated.

The closed letters a and o show his ability to keep secrets.

The speed and connections of the writing show a quick logical mind able to deal promptly with important matters. Obviously he can be argumentative and stubborn when his mind is made up.

The size of Jon's capital letters shows self-respect, self-confidence and pride in his own achievements.

The long lower loops and the occasionally filled-in letters show strong sensual and physical interests.

The arrow dots over the small letters i are a strong feature of his writing. These indicate that he has a natural sense of wit and humour.

An equally startling example of how current thoughts affect handwriting is shown by the sample of writing submitted to me by film star/producer Richard Attenborough (Figure 3). The emotive character of his writing was caused by the subject he was writing about, the distressing disease muscular dystrophy.

I will explain fully how to recognise these dominant clues to a person's moods in later chapters dealing with the basic guides to graphology.

CHAPTER THREE

If you read advertisements for senior executive posts, very often you will see the phrase "Apply in your own handwriting".

This usually means that a consultant graphologist like myself is employed to advise on whether applicants are suited psychologically to handle the job advertised.

It does not surprise me when my character-assessment by graphology of candidates coincides with the opinion of the selection panel who have full access to the technical qualifications of the applicants.

Graphology is used also by lawyers and police to detect forgeries. And firms sometimes use graphology to assess the honesty of their staff—though I must admit I dislike this field and usually I decline such assignments.

Sometimes there is confusion between graphology and calligraphy. For instance, recently in the Michael Parkinson television show Orson Welles described graphology as calligraphy when being used in forgery detection.

He was wrong. Calligraphy is a form of artistic handwriting, which can indicate a degree of self-adoration or it could mean that the writer has a strong artistic appreciation of what is graceful and beautiful.

The point I am making is that there is a very serious side to graphology and there is nothing mysterious about it.

It is a science of principles—by study you can become a doctor . . . by study you can become a graphologist.

If you follow the instructions in the chapters following and study the analyses I have made of the celebrities—all of whom confirm the accuracy of my assessments—you will be able to measure your own abilities in the fascinating and educational field of graphology.

CHAPTER FOUR

The interest in handwriting analysis is nothing new.

Long before the birth of Christ, Chinese philosophers and writers noted the cultural characteristics of their contemporaries by the finesse and artistry of their pictorial and symbolic styles of handwriting.

In the First Century AD the Roman historian Suetonious Tranquillus gave a damning character analysis of one of the Caesar family, Octovious Augustus, by studying his handwriting.

The monks of the Middle Ages, since they were among the few literate people around at the time, studied handwriting and tried to analyse the character of their colleagues and the barons who wielded much power.

In the Eighteenth Century monks had the time and inclination to make a more serious research into graphology and because of the growing literacy in all walks of life their findings have proved to be valuable to historians.

In Britain in the Nineteenth Century some of the great literary personalities of the times, including Edgar Alan Poe, Sir Walter Scott and Charles Dickens, took an active interest in the meaning of graphology.

It seems natural to understand that Poe, the master of horror, had a predilection toward any evil character in handwriting since graphology can expose these tendencies in a person more quickly than any other science.

A trained graphologist can detect a sadist or pervert by studying the person's handwriting.

Sir Walter Scott, a barrister by profession and a writer by desire, was very interested in assessment of the character of people.

In fact he was probably the pioneer of what is now internationally accepted—the final selection of personnel by employing the services of an experienced graphologist.

Let me quote from his "Chronicles from the Canongate", published in 1827:

"There was something in this conclusion which at first reading piqued me extremely and I was so unnatural as to curse the whole concern, as poor, bald, pitiful trash, in which a silly old man was saying a great deal about nothing at all. Nay, my first impression was to thrust it into the fire . . . "

Then after a few lines he continues:

"A little reflection made me ashamed of this feeling of impatience, and as I looked at the even, concise, yet tremulous hand, in which the manuscript was written, I could not help thinking, according to an opinion I have heard seriously maintained, that something of a man's character may be conjectured from his handwriting.

"That neat but crowded and constrained small-hand argued a man of a good conscience, well-regulated passions and to use his own phrase, an upright walk in life, but it also indicated narrowness of spirit, inveterate prejudice, and hinted at some degree of intolerance, which, though not natural to the disposition, had arisen out of a limited education.

"Then the flourished capital letters which ornamented the commencement of each paragraph and the names of his family and of his ancestors whenever these occurred in the page, do they not express forcibly the pride and sense of importance with which the author undertook and accomplished his task?

"I persuaded myself the whole was so complete a portrait of the man, that it would not have been a more undutiful act to have defaced his picture, or even to have disturbed his bones in his coffin, than to destroy his manuscript."

In the Twentieth Century, research took place into the value of handwriting and its analysis.

Graphologists began to adopt a scientific attitude to the subject. Many hundreds of specimens of handwriting by people in known walks of life were gathered and graphic characteristics carefully correlated.

In this way common symbols were found and a basic list of character trends drawn up.

My father, Arthur White, commenced this study shortly after he left the Royal Navy.

During World War I he had collected hundreds of handwriting specimens from shipmates.

Being involved in the hazardous retreats from Antwerp and Gallipoli noted in history books he met men stripped of all falseness, was able to observe them and judge their character. They also

19

gave him specimens of their handwriting or gave him samples of letters from their loved ones.

As a result, by the early Twenties he had amassed a library of more than 20,000 graphological specimens, all of which were backed by personal observation of the persons involved.

He evolved "The White Write System", a method of analysing human character by handwriting.

The accuracy of this system has been proved many times over and you will see for yourself in this book the testimonials from celebrities analysed accurately in recent times by my use of this method.

This system has a simple basis and I hope this will encourage readers to deepen their researches into the science of graphology and also enjoy it as an intriguing hobby.

CHAPTER FIVE

So now we come to the section impatiently awaited by many listeners of Pete Murray's Open House radio programme who take the trouble to write.

How do I analyse so accurately the character of the famous celebrities who appear on the programme?

First, I would like to emphasise that even by earnestly studying the clues given in this book, you will not become an expert graphologist overnight.

I started studying graphology seriously in 1940 and it has taken me since then to reach the degree of accuracy I achieve now.

What I suggest you do is:

(1) Study the graphological pointers I give you.
(2) Read my analyses of the famous celebrities' writing.
(3) Check the points I make in each analysis with the graphological pointer system.
(4) When you feel you have mastered the pointer system, blank out my analyses of the celebrities. Then study their writing and try to make your own analysis. Do this with at least ten of the celebrities' handwriting samples. Then check your findings with mine.

All of these celebrities have confirmed the accuracy of my analyses. So, where you find you disagree with my findings have another look and see where you have gone wrong.

(5) After re-reading the book, re-analyse the same ten celebrities and see if your findings have changed.
(6) If your findings are in line with the stars' major characteristics as analysed by me then carry on.

Ask members of your family to give you a seven-line specimen of their natural handwriting in the form of a letter with their signature.

When they give you the specimens, analyse them as though they were strangers and the resultant analyses should show how quickly you are picking up graphology.

You know their character and if this checks with your analyses then you have achieved some success.

If you do well with your family, you are well on the way to widening your field in graphology and next-door neighbours, boy and girl friends are the obvious next step.

After that, the whole exciting world of graphology is open to you. . . .

CHAPTER SIX

For a successful analysis of handwriting it is essential that the specimen submitted should be the natural writing of the subject. In other words, to get the true assessment of the subject's character the specimen should be written as though he or she was dressed in ordinary everyday clothes, not dressed-up in order to impress other people.

The length of the specimen should not be less than seven lines and preferably these seven lines should be written in the form of a letter. The contents of the letter do not matter, since normally these are incidental in handwriting analysis.

For example two politicians I analysed, the Prime Minister Harold Wilson and Lord Arran, submitted a wealth of material on which I could base my judgement of their character.

In the case of Harold Wilson I was given more than 30 pages of draft speeches written by him over a period of time.

In the case of Lord Arran I was given three books full of his draft articles for the *Evening News*.

Voluminous specimens such as these are extremely valuable and enable a graphologist to judge changes of mood in the writer, how the writer is affected by the subject he is writing about, or how an event of the day has affected his mind.

Two rather vivid examples of this were shown earlier in the book with the writing of Jon Pertwee; how tiredness and the hearing of bad news had affected his normal style of hand-writing.

In the example of the film star **Richard Attenborough** this showed signs of considerable depression by the subject he was writing about.

Once you have received your specimen, you commence your analysis and general assessment by taking into consideration seventeen different points.

These are:

POINTER 1.   a. THE ZONES.
              b. PRESSURE.
POINTER 2.   LETTER LAYOUT.
POINTER 3.   SPACING LAYOUT.
POINTER 4.   SIZE.
POINTER 5.   SLOPE OF THE LINES.
POINTER 6.   SLANT OF THE LETTERS.
POINTER 7.   SHAPE AND EVENNESS OF THE LETTERS.
POINTER 8.   CONNECTION OF THE LETTERS.
POINTER 9.   EXTENSION OF THE WRITING.
POINTER 10.   INITIAL LETTERS OF THE WORDS.
POINTER 11.   FINAL LETTERS OF THE WORDS.
POINTER 12.   CAPITAL LETTERS.
POINTER 13.   THE LETTERS I AND i.
POINTER 14.   THE LETTER T.
POINTER 15.   THE a AND o.
POINTER 16.   THE LOOPS.
              a. UPPER ZONE.
              b. LOWER ZONE.
POINTER 17.   THE SIGNATURE.

During each of these pointers you list your findings and then this list becomes:

POINTER 18, a summary of the features of the handwriting.

Then you go through this summary before making your final analysis.

It may well be that you find there are some conflicting tendencies in the handwriting. Then you should list these clashing tendencies and find out which tendency is dominant in the handwriting. The dominant tendencies are the tendencies that reflect the true character of the subject. It is on this that you base your final analysis.

CHAPTER SEVEN

POINTER 1. a. THE ZONES

The Zones are divided into the upper zone—the upper loops—the middle zone—meaning the middle parts of the letters—and the lower zone—meaning the lower loops of the letters.

Such letters as b, d and h occupy both the upper zone and the middle zone. Whereas f is the only letter of the alphabet that occupies or should occupy all three zones in equal proportions.

Middle Zone

Letters completely in this zone are a, e, o, u—the body portion. In other words the rounded portion of the letter b is in the MIDDLE ZONE, and the stem extends to the UPPER ZONE.

The body zone of the letter y is in the MIDDLE ZONE whereas the lower loop descends to the LOWER ZONE.

Lower Zone

As the name implies the lower zone refers to the lower loops of letters such as g, p, q, y.

MEANING OF ZONE DOMINANCE

In making the general assessment of a handwriting specimen, it is important to see in which zone the dominance is.

If the dominance is in the upper zone it shows that the writer is somewhat of an idealist and holds spiritual values rather strongly.

If the upper zone is unduly high it may indicate the person lives in a world of his or her own.

If there is undue emphasis on the middle zone, in other words the lower loops and upper loops are abnormally small and the middle zone is abnormally large, then it means the person is purely interested in what is happening at the moment.

If the lower loops or lower zone is particularly strong then it shows how down-to-earth the person is and also the physical side of the person.

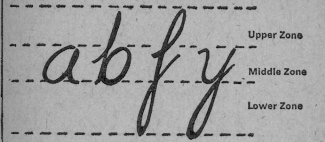

Upper Zone

Middle Zone

Lower Zone

This is light pressure.

This is average pressure.

This is heavy pressure.

The meaning of the upper zone loops and lower loops are dealt with in greater detail in Pointer 16.

POINTER 1. b. Pressure

At one time pressure was one of the most important points in a graphological analysis. This was in the days of fountain pens or other nib pens. A great deal of research was made into the pressure of up-strokes and down-strokes as these denoted character and characteristics.

Since nowadays 90 per cent of the population use ball-point pens, the importance of pressure in a graphological analysis obviously has decreased.

However, it remains a fact that people who use fountain pens usually have more individualistic character than people who use ball-point pens.

And people who use felt-tip pens have a more artistic character than people who use ball pens.

However, it is still possible to gauge pressure of writing, whether the writer uses a fountain pen, felt pen or ball pen.

With fountain pens, people who naturally use light pressure when writing usually choose fine nibs for their pens. If by chance they do use medium nibs then they use these so their writing has a light appearance on the paper.

People with light pressure using a ball pen will give the appearance of just touching the paper and there will be no impression on the back of the page.

People using a felt pen, if they have light pressure, will have open and visible loops in letters such as f. If they use a heavy pressure these loops will be closed in one blob.

Light pressure denotes basically quiet personalities with a dislike of violence. They are usually of a retiring disposition and often have cultural interests in the arts or literature.

Fountain pen users who have heavy pressure normally prefer to use a broad nib.

In the case of a ball pen, heavy pressure can be recognised by the imprint of the writing at the back of the page.

In the case of a felt pen, heavy pressure means that the loops of letters f and g for instance are filled in and other letters are blotchy.

Heavy pressure can denote a nervous tension in the writer. Well-formed heavy pressure writing denotes a strong, artistic sense.

Filled-in loops in both fountain pen and felt pen writing indicates a strongly sensual nature.

CHAPTER EIGHT

POINTER 2. LETTER LAYOUT

This deals with the margins on the letter page and the spacing of the letter as a whole—the spacing between words and the spacing between lines.

Figure 1 is a perfectly balanced letter layout. The margins both left and right are almost equal, the contents of the letter are also perfectly balanced, giving an equal margin to the top and bottom of the page. The spacing between the words and lines are also equally balanced.

This type of layout usually indicates a person with a keen brain and ability to size-up situations. They are usually neat and tidy both in appearance and methods of working. They are not likely to be the type who get in a flap and most likely have considerable business ability, especially if the dots over the letters i are directly above and near the stem.

Figure 2 shows a very narrow left margin and a very wide right margin. This happens often if there is a leftward tendency in the handwriting.

This type of margin distinction indicates people with an element of withdrawal and introversion.

They do not meet other persons easily, and in fact depending on the other characteristics in the handwriting they may actively dislike having to meet and mingle with others. Again this type of person is likely to be very practical.

Figure 3 shows a wide left margin and a very narrow right margin. This person is likely to have characteristics almost directly opposing those of the person of Figure 2 type.

The Figure 3 writer at times may be impractical and impulsive. They usually enjoy meeting people and take a keen interest in the affairs of the world and other communities.

Figure 4 has a left margin which gradually increases as the letter proceeds, and this indicates that writers of this type have an initial lack of self-confidence. However as they warm-up to people or subjects, their confidence increases. This especially is true if the

POINTER 2.

Figure 1.

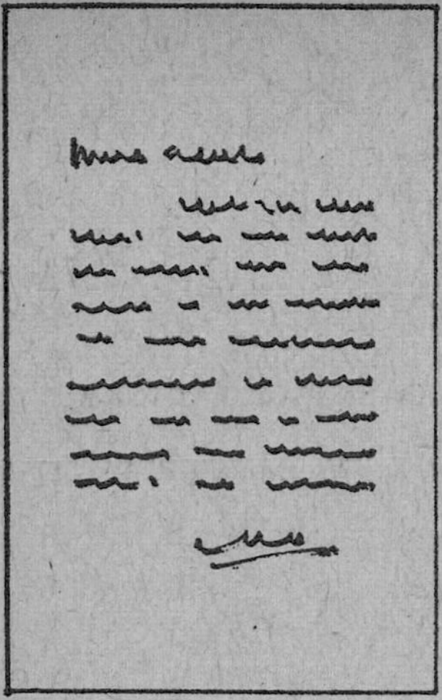

Figure 3.

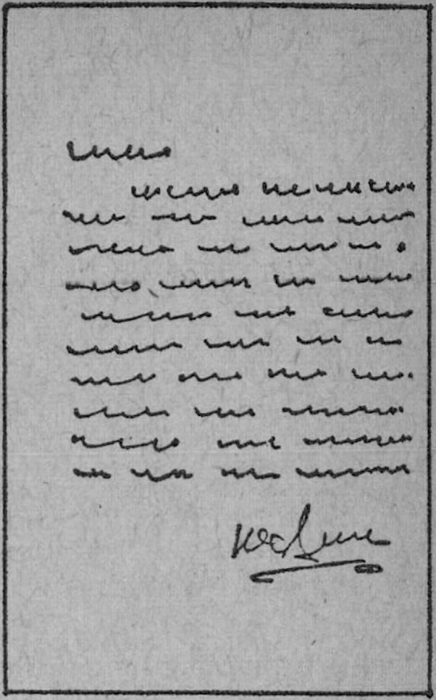

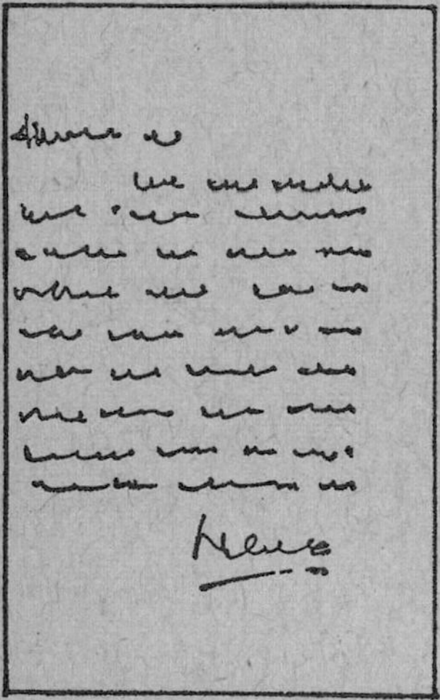

Figure 2.

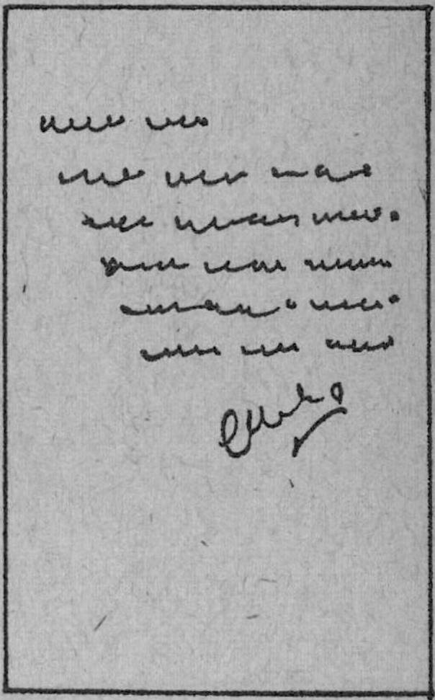

Figure 4.

Figure 5.

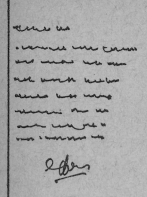

Figure 7.

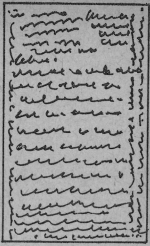

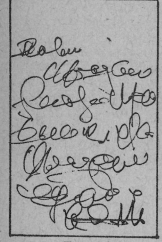

Figure 6.

right margin, at the same time, narrows in sympathy with the left-hand margin's increase.

Figure 5 shows an increasing right margin—the opposite of Figure 4. This type of writer initially may be ready to meet people and feel quite confident but as the meeting progresses there is gradual withdrawal and loss of confidence.

Figure 6 is a specimen with no margins to the left or right of the page. A perfect example of this handwriting is shown later in the book in the specimen of musical star Dolores Gray.

This type of writer usually has an impulsive and generous nature and is the type of person who wants to make use of every minute of life. They are usually of a restless nature.

Figure 7 is of a completed letter in which the writer has used every available piece of margin space left in the letter with extra messages.

This indicates that the person concerned is thoroughly impractical, has no sense of organising either their own lives or that of anyone else.

These writers are most likely to be impractical both in business and domestic affairs. Usually they are completely unable to take a realistic view of things or face up to the realities of the world.

They are likely to be unable to stop talking, even if what they are talking about is sheer triviality. It may also be a sign of loneliness.

CHAPTER NINE

POINTER 3. SPACING LAYOUT

Words and lines in Figure 1 are examples of natural handwriting layout and by themselves they have no particularly significant character features.

Figure 2 shows extremely well-balanced handwriting, with words separated and spacing between the lines all equally uniform. Most of the characteristics referred to in Figure 1 of Pointer 2, apply to this type of handwriting.

Figure 3 is an example of handwriting where the words and letters within the words are entangled. And spacing between the lines also is enmeshed.

This is usually the handwriting of people with minds equally entangled and a complete sense of unreality towards the world. The type of person referred to in Figure 7 of Pointer 2 often adopts this style of handwriting.

If in conjunction with the general jumbling-up of the handwriting, the actual letters within the words jump considerably in size from letter to letter, it can be a sign of mental instability. Almost always this type of handwriting indicates a lack of logical reasoning powers.

On the other hand, it could be the handwriting of a creative genius whose only object in writing is to set down his or her ideas as quickly as possible on paper without any regard to whether any other person will read or understand them.

Again, all other characteristics of the handwriting have to be taken into consideration to decide which category the writer belongs to.

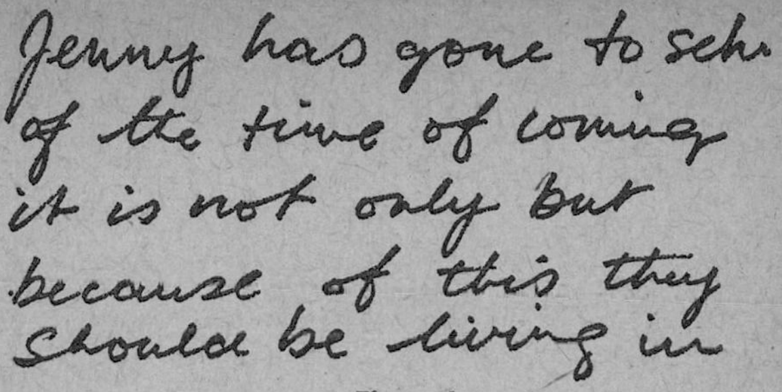

Jenny has gone to sch.
of the time of coming
it is not only but
because of this they
should be living in

Figure 1.

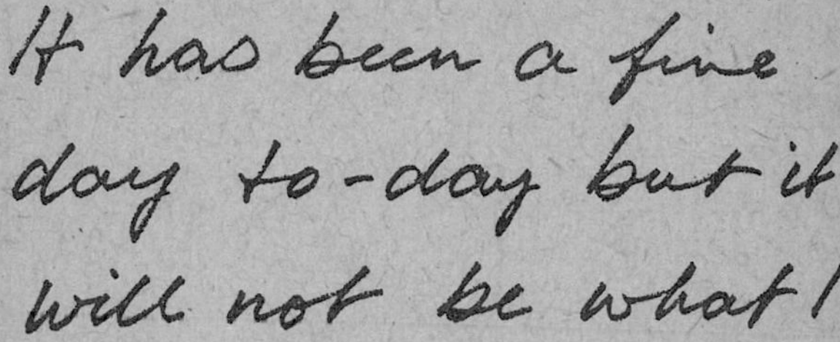

It has been a fine
day to-day but it
will not be what I

Figure 2.

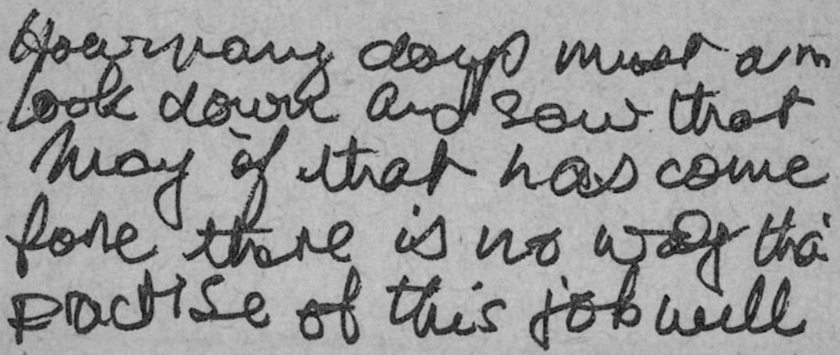

Spearvang days must am
look down and saw that
may of that has come
fore there is no way tha
pactise of this job well

Figure 3.

3

CHAPTER TEN

POINTER 4. SIZE

Figure 1 is extremely small and neat handwriting.

There are two interpretations of the character of this type of person.

The first interpretation is that the person is of well above average intelligence. He probably is engaged in a profession that requires a great deal of research, patience and has an ability to pay attention to details.

The second interpretation is that the person is a complete introvert and lacks confidence in himself or herself.

The only way to get a correct assessment of which category the subject falls into is to compare this characteristic with others given in the later Pointers of this book.

If they fall into the first category, the writing will be extremely small, in fact often in cases of brilliant people it is almost microscopic and unreadable in size.

Under a magnifying glass each letter will be perfectly formed and the spacing between letters and between lines will be perfectly balanced.

The letters within the words almost certainly always are connected and the dot over the stem of the small letter i will be directly above the letter and usually extremely near to the stem.

Again in this category the writer often uses up every inch of the space on the page.

If the writer falls into the second category the writing may slope backwards, the finals of the final letters of each word may hook backwards, sometimes dramatically, and the lower loops are likely to have a decided swing to the left and may not come into a circle back to the right. The right-hand margin of the page is likely to be wider than the left-hand margin.

Figure 2 shows medium-size handwriting and this is average for normal people. As a single factor it has no special significance or characteristic.

POINTER 4.

(1) *this is small writing*

(2) *this is average writing*

(3) *above average size*

Figure 3 is usually used by the type of people who stand out in a crowd. Whether they stand out in a pleasant or unpleasant way you will be able to judge by reading the later Pointers and adding together the characteristics of the rest of the specimen.

Mentally unstable people often write like this, but in general this is the handwriting of a natural showman.

The subject is likely to be full of verve, vivacity and self-importance, or if not self-importance, certainly self-confidence.

Usually this category of subject talks loudly. They enjoy pushing themselves—and pushing others. They are the type who are likely to give a retiring person a hearty slap on the back and say "Go on, push yourself forward and do not be so modest". They are likely to have physical strength and plenty of mental energy . . .

Curiously enough, although they may have physical strength, it is unlikely they will have any physical prowess in competitive sport.

I have analysed the character of dozens of the world's top sporting celebrities and not one has had this size of handwriting.

If the handwriting is abnormally large—in other words a few millimetres more than the specimen illustrated—and the actual pressure of the writing is thick, the formation of the letters is ugly and the loops of letters such as f and g are filled-in with ink, then beware of this person.

CHAPTER ELEVEN

POINTER 5. SLOPE OF THE LINES

Figure 2 is the horizontal level which is written by the average writer. This characteristic again means nothing in itself.

Figure 1 shows an extremely upward trending slope of the lines and an admirable example of this is shown later in the book in the specimens of handwriting submitted to me by pianist Liberace.

This type of writer is usually full of driving force, energy and is supremely optimistic.

They are the types who can take the rough with the smooth and do not give up easily.

You usually will find that this type of writer falls into the same category as the writer in Pointer 2, Figure 3, and possesses the same characteristics.

Figure 3 is where the writer proceeds on normal horizontal levels until near the end of the lines when the words suddenly begin to droop.

There are several interpretations of this which necessitate your studying the other Pointers in the book and finding the characteristics applied to the interpretations that can be made with this style of handwriting. For example:

(a) It can be written by persons in normal health writing in their normal fashion, but they are extremely tired at the time of writing and the handwriting just comes to a slight droop.

However they pull themselves together again for the next line of handwriting and carry on writing horizontally until near the end of the line, tiredness overtaking them again. If they are really exhausted the general slope is likely to continue downwards quite dramatically.

(b) If the words on the line basically are in a straight horizontal line but each word droops slightly downwards, it shows again extreme tiredness but the writing is done with a determination to carry on.

This individual word drooping shows a degree of tiredness more than (a) and the writers may well be overtaxing their energies.

POINTER 5.

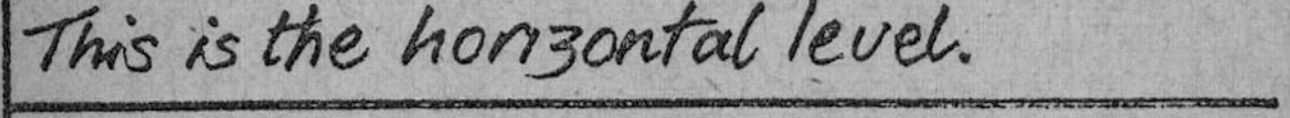
This is the horizontal level.

Figure 2.

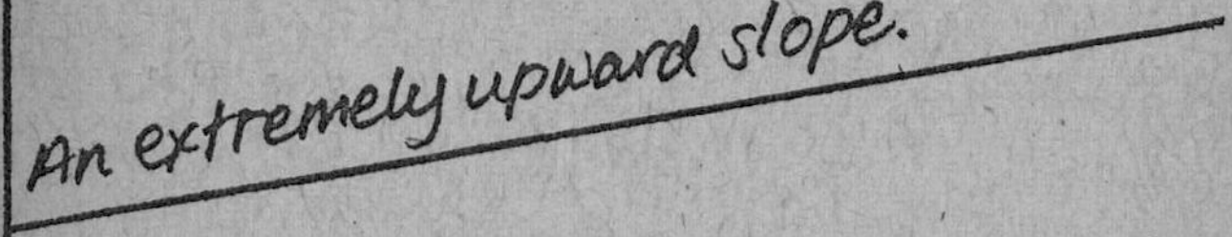
An extremely upward slope.

Figure 1.

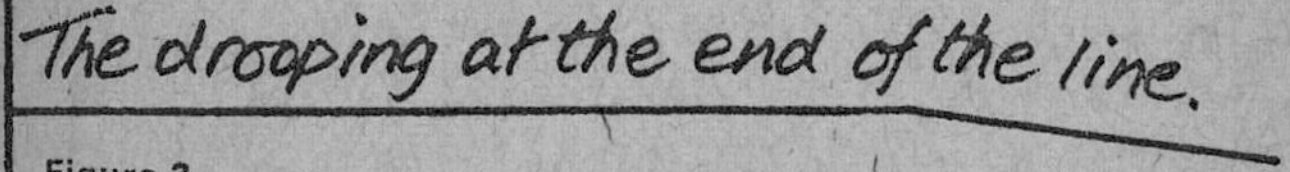
The drooping at the end of the line.

Figure 3.

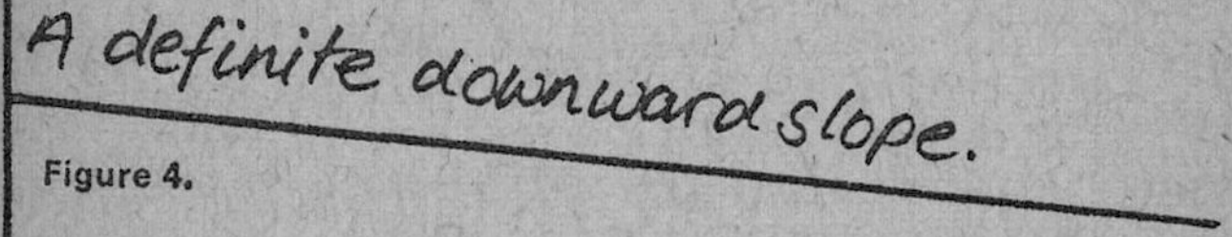
A definite downward slope.

Figure 4.

(c) If each word in the line and each letter within the word has shaky formation it indicates a physical ill-health.

If each word is slanting slightly upward it shows that the writer is making a very determined effort to overcome the ill-health.

Likewise, if each word gradually dips then it points to the writer fighting a battle.

Regarding characteristics like this I must emphasise that readers should not jump to hasty conclusions until they are more qualified in the science of graphology. It takes years of experience to diagnose those elements of physical illness in handwriting.

Figure 4 is where the handwriting has a definite downward slant. A perfect example of this is shown in the samples in this book of Richard Attenborough's handwriting.

I must repeat that when a lay or amateur graphologist finds this specimen of handwriting on no account must he or she jump to conclusions.

The writing may simply reflect the immediate mood of the writer. It may be that something has happened that day that has affected them personally. Or it may be that the subject they are writing about at the time is having an influence upon them. Their normal handwriting may be average. However if there is a sudden variation of slope of the lines as in this instance then it shows the writer has a strong sense of idealism and can become extremely emotional when events take place that upset these ideals.

However, if you get several specimens of handwriting written by the same person on different dates and all slanting down at the angle given in Figure 4 then you may be certain that this is the writing of a thoroughly depressed person who has little interest in either himself or herself or in anyone else.

CHAPTER TWELVE

POINTER 6. SLANT OF THE LETTERS

You do not need to be a graphologist to know that there are three main slants of handwriting: the backward handwriting, sloping toward the left; the upright perpendicular handwriting and frontward right-sloping handwriting.

Left sloping handwriting could be classified as handwriting which slants backwards at an angle of anything from 85 degrees downwards.

Perpendicular handwriting can be taken as handwriting in which the slant is between 85 and 95 degrees.

Rightward sloping handwriting can be classed as handwriting which slopes from 95 degrees forward.

For many years graphologists have agreed that the average slant of handwriting is between 105 and 115 degrees. However I hesitate to class these angles as the average slant of modern-day handwriting.

In the first 8 weeks I was on the Pete Murray "Open House" show, I received more than 5,000 letters from listeners and I was able to make a survey of these letters to find the dominant slant of handwriting.

Of course most of these letters must have been from housewives, but it is a graphological fact that it is impossible to judge the sex of the writer by handwriting alone.

Another long-discarded theory is that all men write with a right-ward slant and all women write with a leftward slant.

Anyway the result of the survey showed that of the 5,000 letters 55 per cent were in perpendicular handwriting; 25 per cent were left-sloping; and 20 per cent were right-sloping.

In a much smaller survey of known male handwriting I found the figures to be: 50 per cent perpendicular; 35 per cent right-sloping; and 15 per cent left-sloping.

While these figures seem to confirm that more women than men tend to write with a leftward slant the one conclusive result is that the average style nowadays clearly is the upright perpendicular slant.

I believe this swing from the rightward slant to the perpendicular slant is caused by three facts:

(1) That nowadays people take less pride in the style of their handwriting.

(2) The decline of fountain pens and the advent of ball pens. While the shape of fountain pen nibs allowed greater ease of writing by use of the rightward slant, ball pens can write at any angle (which does not necessarily add artistry to handwriting).

(3) That in schools less importance than before is given to getting pupils to write with a rightward slant. In fact, in general the standard of handwriting education in schools is deplorable. Handwriting once classed as semi-illiterate could now almost be described as the average handwriting of school-leavers.

Figure 1. Leftward Slant: This means that the writer has some introversion in his or her nature. This may vary from reticence to extreme timidity depending on the degree of the backward slant, from 85 down to 70 degrees.

Approximately 70 degrees would be the line of reticence, but below this indicates considerable timidity and perhaps almost a fear of meeting people.

People with a backward slant are not normally naturally good mixers. This either may be the cause of an inherent shyness or that they genuinely prefer their own company and a small circle of close friends.

They usually are extremely loyal to their friends and sometimes quite possessive. With younger writers it may indicate a degree of sexual repression or job frustration. With older writers it can indicate a degree of disappointment at unfulfilled ambitions.

Figure 2. The Upward or Perpendicular Slant: This is a slant where writing is at the angles of 85 to 95 degrees. As I stated earlier this used to be recognised as a slant behind the average handwriting. According to the old graphological diagnosis, this indicated a degree of coldness in character and scepticism and a preoccupation with the present and less interest in the future.

I would say in present times this indicates a general scepticism about the future—in the world and in domestic life.

In recent years, despite promises of prosperity there has been one crisis after another and not much progress seems to be made. So I would say that now this slant is an indication of people's attitudes to politicians' and leaders' promises . . . in other words the average person now has a mood of caution. They are not so idealistic as they used to be about the future.

Some may be more fatalistic than others and the degree of this outlook can be judged by the other characteristics in the handwriting.

Generally speaking, the persons with the handwriting of the 85 to 90 degrees are likely to be more pessimistic than those with the 90 to 95 degrees angles of handwriting.

People with writing at this slant usually take a calm view of the scene and are unlikely to rush into any decisions without consideration of the situation.

Persons with this angle of writing usually have a certain lack of warmth of feeling. They are more likely to be analytical, sometimes coldly analytical, in their assessment of people and affairs.

They are unlike people with the leftward slant in as much as they rely on their own judgement and are certainly not afraid of meeting people or facing the opinions of other people.

Although they may have a certain aloofness, they are usually good judges of character. They are the type of people that those with the extreme leftward and extreme rightward writing slants run to in cases of emergency.

Figure 3. 95 degrees onward.

Up to 100 degrees the personality of the writer can be taken as average. They have quite a free outlook and are rather inclined to take things as they come. Unless there are certain other characteristics and other points in their handwriting they are able to solve problems by logical reasoning.

Figure 4. 100 degrees onward.

Generally these writers look on the brighter side of things and are full of enthusiasm and energy and are keen to meet people. The greater the degree of slant the more they take obstacles in their stride. If there also is a narrow right margin it shows a great interest in meeting people and in the affairs of the world.

If the handwriting slopes to an extreme degree of 130 degrees or over it shows a complete reckless nature and gullibility.

POINTER 6.

Figure 1.

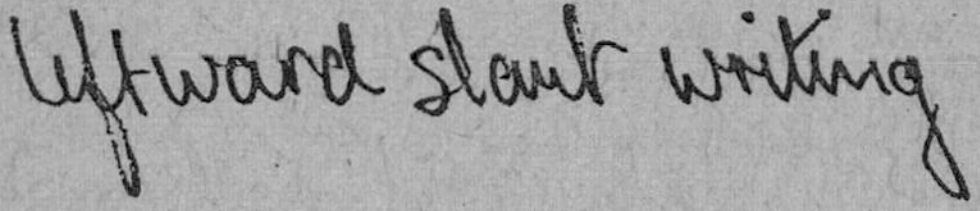
leftward slant writing

Figure 2.

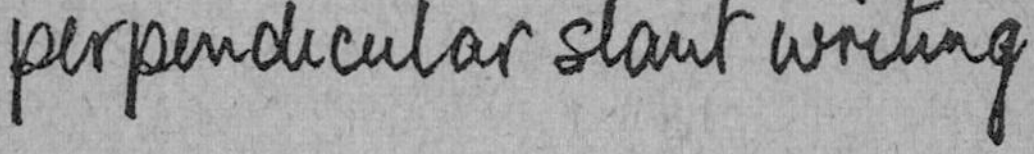
perpendicular slant writing

Figure 3.

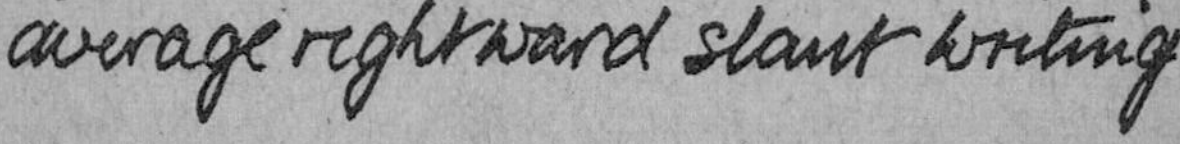
average rightward slant writing

Figure 4.

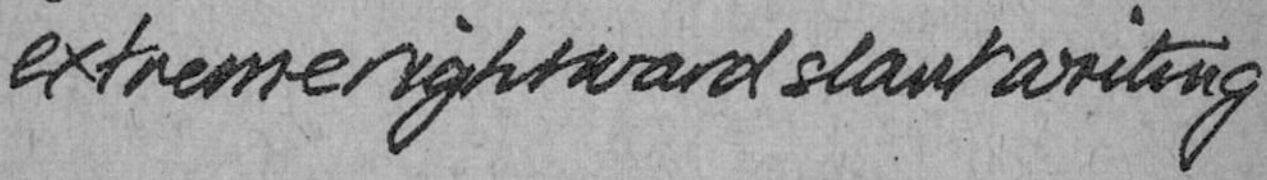
extreme rightward slant writing

CHAPTER THIRTEEN

POINTER 7. SHAPE AND EVENNESS OF THE LETTERS

The shape of the letters is sometimes called "the connection of the letters" by other graphologists. I think that this is rather misleading and the term "connection of the letters" I feel is better to refer to the actual linking of letters between words. Consequently I follow this chapter with Pointer 8, "Connection of the Letters".

There are four main shapes of letters to be taken into consideration for character analysis. Where the handwriting of the specimen does not fall into any of these categories, it indicates it is average-shaped handwriting and in itself means little in assessment of character.

The Angular Shape is shown in Figure 1.

To some, this style of handwriting may appear sharp and ugly, but it reveals an incisive and decisive character both mentally and creatively.

Such people are usually strong-minded, strong-willed and are determined to push through their own ideas. It is found frequently in the writing of hard-selling salesmen, and creative people in advertising such as copywriters and visualisers.

It also is found in the writing of individual designers and architects whose main job is to produce an essentially practical product or project.

This style does have a ruthless appearance and this is quite often reflected in the character of the person using it. They are full of energy and enthusiasm and will spare no one, not even themselves, to achieve their ends.

Figure 2 shows the Garland Shape.

This is almost a direct opposite to the angular handwriting. The gentle flowing base of the letters are restful to the eyes, and this reflects the image of the person.

Garland-style writers usually have an easy-going nature and are of gentle disposition. They dislike getting involved in any disagreements.

Being of a highly sensitive disposition, they are often taken

POINTER 7

FIG 1.   ANGULAR

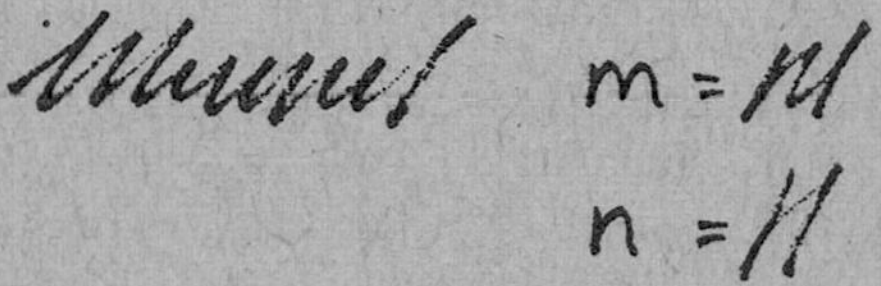

ıllumul $m = \mathcal{M}$

$n = /\!/$

FIG 2.   GARLAND

uuuuu $m = \mathcal{u}\mathcal{u}$

$n = \mathcal{u}$

FIG 3.   ARCADE

mmm $m = m$

$n = n$

FIG 4.   THREAD

b⎯⎯⎯⎯⎯ $= THREAD$

advantage of by persons who have an angular style of handwriting.

Usually garland-style writers do not see the point of standing up for opinions they hold. Because they take the line of least resistance, they often easily are swayed in their judgement. Usually their attitude is anything for a quiet life.

Such writers are generally creative and spiritually minded. Many of the best musical composers and poetic writers have this type of script.

The degree of gentleness and even submissiveness of character in the garland writer is best seen in the formation of the letters m and n.

When these appear to look like the letters w and u, you have an extreme garland-style writer. Writers of this style are usually of a very sympathetic nature and are good friends to have. They generally have a very trusting nature.

The Arcade Shape is in Figure 3.

This visually is the complete opposite to garland handwriting. In the case of arcade, the tops of the letters are rounded in an arch formation. The small letter n rather resembles the arched back of a cat when confronted with an attacking dog. Rather like cats arcade writers are basically "loners". They often hold their own opinions and tend to stick by these. They are not easily persuaded by other people's arguments.

Like the garland writers, they have an excellent creative sense but their creation usually is more on the practical and structural side.

They usually have an excellent sense of form and perspective.

In this category of handwriting, frequently there can be found industrial designers and architects who are involved in products of elegant design and buildings of visual beauty.

Thread Shape is in Figure 4.

Beginners in graphology should be careful before they try to make an analysis of thread-shaped handwriting; it has several interpretations.

This writing is of a style that is almost indecipherable. Before making a character analysis it is essential to find out if it is the person's normal handwriting or whether it is just because of the condition he or she is in.

People who have had too much to drink often resort to this style of writing when they are trying to make notes. Since handwriting is brainwriting this is a vivid example of the brain being unable to operate.

Curiously enough, in the cold light of the day such writers are able to decipher their own notes even when these are completely indecipherable to others.

If this is the normal style of handwriting of the people being analysed, then this is the type of person with whom to be careful.

If there are other confirmative characteristics in the handwriting, this can indicate that the writers are hiding something.

Either the writers have no faith in themselves, or they are shrewd and diplomatic even to the point of deception and untruthfulness.

On the more positive side, this style can indicate that the writers do not give a damn what others think since they have a complete sense of self-preoccupation.

*   *   *

THE AVERAGE EVENNESS OF LETTERS

This is of no special significance on its own and simply indicates that the writer is average and ready to accept the normal routine of life.

UNBALANCED LETTERS

Usually this type of writer is either not particularly bright or literate, or is the type of person who finds it difficult to collate his or her thoughts. Their minds seem to be too jumbled-up with ideas.

This is particularly true if the lower loops of the lines entangle with the zone of the following line of handwriting.

In addition to letters being completely uneven, if the base line of the handwriting bobs up and down it usually is a sign of either mental instability or some form of illness.

Once again I would like to emphasise to amateur graphologists not to jump to conclusions on samples such as these. It is much better to concentrate on the other characteristics of the handwriting.

DESCENDING LETTERS IN THE WORDS

Where the letters gradually descend toward the end of each word it indicates basically a concealment of facts.

Another interpretation of this characteristic is that the writer is endeavouring to avoid hurting the feelings of the reader.

A cruel interpretation is that the writer deliberately is giving an untrue picture of a person or a situation. Perhaps it is not surprising that quite a number of politicians and journalists have this characteristic in their handwriting.

CHAPTER FOURTEEN

POINTER 8. CONNECTION OF THE LETTERS

Connection of the letters means the linking of individual letters between words, and, in certain cases the linking of the end letter of one word to the initial letter of the next word.

If the letters within the words are linked together making a continual flow it reflects that the writer's mind operates in a similar way . . . there is a continuous flow of logical thought.

If this flow extends from one word to another, in other words if the words are linked together, it shows an even faster flow of thought.

The writer has an extremely creative mind. This particular characteristic appears frequently in the hand of journalists.

An example of this can be seen in the example of handwriting by Marjorie Proops, later in this book.

It also can indicate that the writer has conservative tastes and is a stickler for principles. This is shown in the writing of Christopher Lee and he later confirmed that this was indeed part of his character.

Where individual letters within the word are constantly broken it indicates a person full of nervous energy and intuition. Two vivid specimens of this type of writing appear in later pages in the analyses of Bruce Forsyth and Larry Grayson.

CHAPTER FIFTEEN

POINTER 9. EXTENSION OF WRITING

This refers to the width of individual letters within the words. These widths are placed in the categories: (a) Narrow; (b) Average; (c) Wide.

(a) Narrow.

Angular writers frequently fall into this category. Usually this type of writer has sharp creative ideas which they are prepared to push forward regardless of opposition.

The narrower the handwriting is in comparison to the normal width the more ruthless and self-centred is the writer.

The more rounded form of letter formation in which this narrow characteristic occurs usually indicates caution, self-interest and either a lack of desire to communicate with others or a genuine inability to do so.

(b) Average.

This is the average width of handwriting. As a single factor it means little graphologically.

(c) Wide.

People using this style of writing usually have a convivial nature and enjoy meeting people. Apart from being basically generous, they often may be of an extravagant nature. This particular characteristic can be checked upon by noting the length of the finals of the word and letters.

CHAPTER SIXTEEN

POINTER 10. INITIAL LETTERS OF THE WORDS

Graphologically, initial letters reveal the time it takes writers to put their ideas on paper.

If initial letters at the beginning of sentences start with long flourishes and the initial letters in subsequent words within the sentences have no flourish this indicates that the writers think first about the subjects of the sentences before proceeding without further ado.

If there are flourishes of initial strokes of words within sentences, it is an indication of slow thinking and procrastination.

If there are no initial loops or flourishes in the initial letters of the sentences or on any of the initial letters of words within the sentences, it shows that the writers are quick thinkers and like to put their thoughts down on paper without deliberation.

POINTER 11. FINAL LETTERS OF THE WORDS

The graphological meanings and interpretations of finals of the words can be compared with two people who are just about to part company.

Either they give no handshake, a distant handshake, a weak handshake, or a warm handshake. These gestures reflect the feeling they have toward each other.

So it is with finals of letters in words. Just as handshakes reveal the physical reaction of people to parting, so the final letters of words in writing indicate the feeling of the writers to other people.

Just as there are many styles in physical partings, there are many styles of graphological endings to words. In order not to confuse readers with too many styles I have selected the most common and significant ones for publication here.

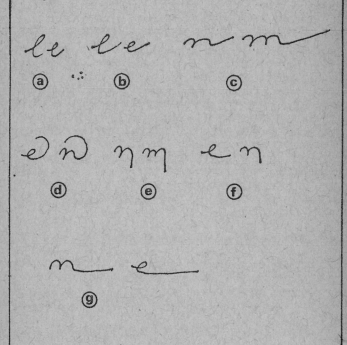

(a)   Practical, self-sufficient.
(b)   Generous, courteous nature.
(c)   Extreme generosity, extravagance.
(d)   Protective nature towards self and others.
(e)   Strong opinions, inclined to be dogmatic.
(f)   As (e) but likely to display temper.
(g)   Strong-minded and suspicious nature.

CHAPTER SEVENTEEN

POINTER 12. CAPITAL LETTERS

It is dangerous to over-emphasise the character of capital letters as a single factor in handwriting analysis. The appearance of capital letters must be taken in context with the characteristics shown in the rest of the specimens submitted.

For instance, if you saw a man walking in the street wearing spectacular clothes like those of Liberace you might make your own instant judgement of him. However, without knowing why the man decided to wear this particular style of clothing your judgement could be completely wrong.

So seek the full facts before judging ornate capital letters in handwriting—they can have several meanings.

Ornate capitals can be the sign of natural showmanship.

They can be the sign of a person full of artistic tendencies and fashion appreciation.

They can be the sign of a person who wishes to brighten-up what he or she thinks is rather a dull world.

The only way to find which category flamboyant capitals writers come within is to check with other points in the analyses.

An excellent example of natural showmanship combined with the desire to cheer the world is found in the handwriting of Liberace. It also is found in the handwriting of Sally Ann Howes and Dolores Gray.

It is not so much the flourish and design of capital letters are so important, it is the shape of the capital letters.

CHAPTER EIGHTEEN

POINTER 13. THE LETTERS I AND i

This Pointer deals with the formation of the capital I letters and the placing of the dot over the small i letters.

It seems to have been proved conclusively by psychologists that the letter I or the spoken word I is the ultimate sign of ego.

In other words it is a sign of how much importance the person attaches to himself.

Just as in conversation when a person repeatedly uses and emphasises the word "I", so in writing if a person consistently uses the word I and emphasises the letter i it indicates considerable self-interest and conceit.

The formation of the capital letter I tends to indicate the confidence a person has in himself. And the placing of the dot over the stem of the small letter i indicates the writer's outlook and aptitude.

(a) **CAPITALS**
(a) Modesty and simplicity.
(b) Practical and businesslike outlook.
(c) Self-pride and confidence.
(d) Self-interest and lack of confidence.

(b) **SMALL LETTERS**
(a) Procrastination, hesitant.
(b) Careless at times.
(c) Orderly.
(d) Very precise and accurate.
(e) Curiosity and enquiring mind.
(f) Enthusiasm.
(g) Natural quick wit and humour.
(h) Strength of character.
(i) Uncertainty of purpose or desire to focus attention to self.

THE LETTER I

(a) CAPITALS

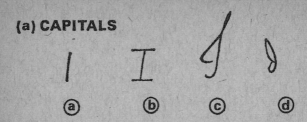

ⓐ   ⓑ   ⓒ   ⓓ

(b) SMALL LETTERS

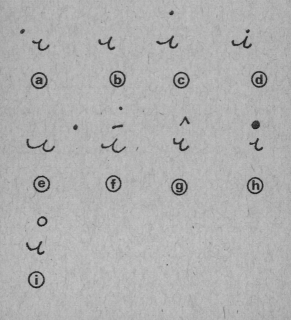

ⓐ   ⓑ   ⓒ   ⓓ

ⓔ   ⓕ   ⓖ   ⓗ

ⓘ

CHAPTER NINETEEN

POINTER 14. THE LETTERS T

The reason that the crosses on letters T and t assume such importance in graphology is that they indicate the amount of energy and enthusiasm of writers.

Basically the stronger the crosses, the stronger the writer. The weaker the crosses, the weaker the writer.

The crosses indicate which category of strength or weakness the writer falls into. Just as an athlete physically may be strong yet weak-willed, so an intellectual may be physically weak yet mentally strong-willed.

As in the section on Finals, I am restricting the illustrations in this section to the type of t stroke or cross most commonly found and most significant.

(a) Natural personality.
(b) Enthusiastic, sometimes impulsive.
(c) Delays taking actions or decisions.
(d) Energetic and ambitious.
(e) As d but more so.
(f) Tenacity and determination.
(g) A hot or strong temper.
(h) Imaginative.
(i) Modesty.
(j) Self depreciatory and sometimes lack of confidence.
(k) Sparky temper with no grudges.
(l) Inclined to be possessive and self-centred.

A

B

C

D

E

F

G

H

I

J

K

L

CHAPTER TWENTY

POINTER 15. THE A AND O

The main graphological interest in the letters a and o is that at school people were taught always to close these. Yet in later life writers have a tendency either to open the tops of these letters, or keep them closed, or tightly knot the connection of the top part of the small letter to the next word.

The continental school of graphologists in the Thirties, laid great store on the factor of the letters a and o being broken at the base. This was an indication of dishonesty, they decided.

Having analysed several hundred such specimens and having checked on the writers, I consider to be invalid this so-called clue to dishonesty.

I find that writers with breaks on the lower sections of the letters a and o usually show signs of break in other parts of letters and have other irregularities in the formation of their handwriting.

I find that the majority of these people are under mental tension or are suffering from physical illness. Certainly in my experience it is not a definite indication of dishonesty or criminal tendencies.

During my career I have had the opportunity to analyse the handwriting of many convicted criminals and I have not found one with the characteristic of having an open base to the letters a and o.

CHAPTER TWENTY-ONE

POINTER 16. THE LOOPS

(a) Upper Zone.
(b) Lower Zone.

The meaning of the upper zone loops and the lower zone loops was described in Pointer 1 relating to the zones of handwriting, so I will go straight into the interpretations of the illustrations given in this section.

(UPPER ZONE)
(a) Spiritual refinement and idealism.
(b) As (a) but inclined to be humble and self-effacing.
(c) Healthy outgoing nature.

(LOWER ZONE)
(a) Healthy outgoing nature.
(b) Physical strength.
(c) Down-to-earth, inclined to be reticent and sometimes suspicious.
(d) Down-to-earth, sometimes fatalistic outlook, dislikes beating about the bush.
(e) Lack of physical strength, sometimes timidity.
(f) Coldness of nature or sharpness of temper.
(g) Unusual or strong sexual interests.
(h) Sensuality and/or artistic tendencies.

LOOPS
(upper zone)

ⓐ   ⓑ   ⓒ

(lower zone)

ⓐ   ⓑ   ⓒ

ⓓ   ⓔ   ⓕ

ⓖ   ⓗ

CHAPTER TWENTY-TWO

POINTER 17. THE SIGNATURE

The first point I wish to make strongly is that it is absolutely impossible to give a character analysis of a person by his signature alone.

The meaning of a signature can be accurately assessed only by comparison with the body matter of the natural handwriting of the writer.

There are three types of signatures:

AVERAGE—The signature that is found in letters for example written by parents to children or communications between people of other natural human relationships.

BUSINESS SIGNATURES—The type used by business people who sign a considerable number of letters or cheques.

Usually this type of signature appears either in a style that pleases the writer or in a style that is found to be quick or is a form of disguise or illegibility designed to make it difficult to forge.

SYMBOLIC SIGNATURES—These usually are found in the signatures of celebrities in either the sporting world or in show business.

These stars usually try to find the most pleasing design of signature that they feel suits their talents.

Two excellent examples of symbolic signatures are shown in this book in the handwriting of **Perry Como** and **Liberace.**

STARS UNDER THE MICROSCOPE

Hundreds of world-famous personalities have come under the handwriting microscope of Fraser White.

Now he tells you of the personality clues to some of these celebrities as divulged to him by their handwriting.

He explains how to use the advice he already has given to study the style, fluency and pressure of handwriting in a manner that will reveal even inner secrets.

First study each sample of handwriting and come to your own conclusions. Then compare your notes with each analysis by Fraser White.

Once you find you have come to similar conclusions about the stars as shown in the following pages you will know you have gained an intriguing talent for seeking out personal details of people by their writing.

RICHARD ATTENBOROUGH

Normally the contents of any specimen submitted to a graph-ologist has little to do with the actual analysis of the handwriting. However, in this case it played an important part in the analysis, otherwise a completely wrong interpretation could have been arrived at.

The dominant feature of this specimen is the pronounced down-ward slant of the lines of the letters. This shows that at the time of writing the writer was in a mood of strong depression.

Yet other factors in the writing indicate that the subject normally is not likely to have a depressed and fatalistic outlook: there is such driving force in the writing.

Examination of the contents gives a clue. The writer is depressed and feeling frustrated about the failure to find a cure for the terrible affliction muscular dystrophy and anguish is reflected by the downward slant of the lines.

The high upper zone shows the writer's idealism and interest in the social affairs of the world.

Yet the writer is no daydreamer. The hooked back ending to the t cross and the long downstrokes with smallish loops indicate a down-to-earth materialistic view and an excellent business sense.

The downward stroke of the finals confirm a determined nature and strongly-held opinions which the writer is not afraid to express.

There are signs of temper and impatience in this handwriting.

The simplification of the letters shows that the writer likes to get down to brass tacks.

Artistic nature is shown by the sensual strength and pressure of the writing.

The placing of the t crosses to the right and the shape and strength of the i dots indicates energy and enthusiasm.

as another we have to

re for muscular dystrophy . .

an only find it if we are

aise sufficient money to contin

our research. There are seve

nty thousand parents in thi

living constantly in the one

t a cure will be found

5

The perpendicular slope of the writing shows the subject has good reasoning power and keen judgement.

A marked feature of the writing is the frequent disconnection of the letters within the words. This reveals a creative side in which decisions are arrived at hastily and instinctively with plenty of imagination and ideas. Some may misfire, but most are successful.

The writer forms likes and dislikes on first impressions. The small size of writing shows ability to size up a situation quickly and correctly. This also shows keen perception and a highly-developed critical sense.

The marked tendency of letters in the words to taper shows the writer can drive a hard bargain; is extremely shrewd and when the situation demands can be diplomatic and subtle, even insincere. Quite a few politicians have this feature in their handwriting.

On the other hand the frequently open letters a and o show that at other times the writer can be very frank and often tactless.

A dominant feature of this writing is the Greek-shaped d which confirms imaginative nature and an interest in cultural subjects.

The left-looping of letters f shows fluency of thought and a quick mind. Heavy dotting of the letters i shows a strong will.

The t crosses to the right show enthusiasm, energy and liveliness.

the littered wreckage which we had heard and seen literally a thousand times in the last twenty years — all the dreary panoply of disaster was displayed with all the dreary irrelevant detail.

Why? Are all news-writers so devoid of news-sense that they cannot tell a story from a non-story? The only people concerned — and all too intimately concerned — were the victims and their relations. The circumstances (no body knew what they were anyway) were of no conceivable interest.

And yet the newspapers made it item one. Really one despairs of the whole

JOHN ALDERTON

Emphasis of this writing is on the upper and lower zones. This indicates that the subject is of contrasting natures.

There is the spiritual side which is idealistic and somewhat day-dreaming. The lower zone shows a 'down-to-earth outlook, athletic ability and strong sexual drive.

Narrow, sharp formation of the letters shows a sharp mind with creative talent.

The extremely wide spacing between words and lines indicates a liking to have things and affairs in a neat and orderly fashion.

Although the size of the capital letters shows considerable self-confidence in some matters, the low crossing of the letters t indicates humility and modesty.

I've never been

as in any life

can tell by the s...

...ing.

with me...

GORDON BANKS

The most noticeable feature of this specimen is the upward slant of the lines. It shows enthusiasm and optimism and confirms that the writer is hard to discourage.

Formation of the letters shows the sharp and alert mind of a quick and logical thinker.

The very narrow right margin shows an interest in people and what is going on in the world.

Short finals indicate a practical outlook in life and lack of gullibility. The writer is good at assessing people and is not likely to be taken in.

The high upper zone indicates idealism and illustrates a type who is not content to rest with the present and is always thinking about and looking forward to the future.

The knotted f shows an inclination to be secretive and you can be sure the writer knows when to keep a closed mouth.

On the other hand there are characteristics which show a moderate aggression and ability to speak loud and clear when necessary.

The i dots to the right confirms a strong sense of curiosity.

The strong t crosses show determination.

come along to t

forward to me

So take of yo

many thanks

Yours Sincerely

Gordon Beath

_____

The contents of this letter almost frightened me off doing the analysis! Still I will take a chance.

The strong rightward slant indicates a sincere and affectionate nature not given to pomposity.

Speed of the writing and letter connections show a clear and logical thinker. There are frequent breaks showing quick ideas and intention.

The i dots directly over the stems shows a liking to be precise and accurate.

Shape of the d indicates a sensitivity to criticism.

Shape of the t crosses indicates a desire to lead a settled life and a dislike of change for the sake of change.

Formation of the capitals indicates credulity.

Dear Fraser

I think,
tell you, ever
that I'm not r
For a long tin
identity secret
now that you k
die. I'm reali

PATRICK CARGILL

The level base line in combination with the evenness of the small letters and the closed letters a and o shows loyalty, sincerity and tact.

Upright slope of the letters shows a level head, an analytical mind and good reasoning.

Occasional breaks in the words show flashes of intuition and the shape of the letters suggest definite creative abilities as a writer.

The shape shows the writer to be good-natured and peace-loving. Fights and serious arguments are avoided if possible and the line of least resistance is taken. However sensible debates and discussions are enjoyed.

The high stem of the small letters shows modesty and considerable dignity.

Balanced layout of the letter shows a neat and tidy mind. There is likely to be a good taste in fashion, furnishings and an appreciation of colours and colour schemes.

The small letters of the signature are in almost the same style and size as the letters in the body of the letter which combined with the formation of the capital letters confirms a general modesty and modest self-confidence.

of my handwriting
ll be able to deduce
iaiacter. How very
of you!

I look forward
result on Pete's
next Friday.

Yours sincerely,

Patrick Cargill.

ANDREW CRUICKSHANK

Widely-spaced writing with a noticeable upper slant to the lines indicates the writer has a generally optimistic nature which prefers to look at the brighter side of life.

Extremely simplified capital letters shows a quick mind and the ability to get to the core of any problems. There also is the ability to size up a situation quickly and usually correctly.

The t crosses to the right show enthusiasm and energy and the hook at the end shows determination and tenacity. It would take a lot to happen before this writer admits defeat on any important matter.

The i dots far to the right of the stem show an inquiring mind and strong powers of observation.

Shape of the writing indicates that the subject does not like to be bothered by trivialities and tends to ignore these when they crop up.

Fraser,

On this life

and . you greetings

, as you are w

tie — what I

blot it any way.

I wishes

VIOLET CARSON

This handwriting shows a surprisingly dual character. The very strong materialistic side is almost equally balanced by the creative tendencies.

The perpendicular slope of the letters with a distinct leftward tendency shows a degree of introversion. The writer is not given to display emotions and rather tends to bottle these.

There is an excellent analytical mind with good reasoning powers and judgement.

This type of writing often indicates creative ability, and in this case the creative trait is doubly confirmed by the connection and shape of the writing.

While there is overall connection of the letters within words, there also is quite a number of breaks. This means that while the writer is a natural reasoner and never makes up a mind hastily on matters of real importance, there are plenty of sudden ideas and flashes of intuition most of which prove to be worthwhile.

The shape of the letters reveals a softer and more romantic nature. This is shown by the garland formation where the small letters are rounded at the base; the small letters m look like the letters w and the small letters n look like the letters u.

This shows that the writer is at most times good natured and peace-loving and tries to avoid all fights and arguments. However if becoming involved in disputes a good personal account is given.

There are cultural interests and most likely the writer is fond of the best in art and music and a definite creative ability is shown in these fields.

The materialistic side of the writer's nature is shown again by the strong pressure of the writing. There is strong will-power and great perseverance.

The shortness of the upper strokes of the small letters d indicate a tendency to become very quiet and taciturn at times.

White,

There are obvious
ways to spell your name
— right in both cases.
a letter from me. — isn't
ing. — even if I am to
- as a result. — Something
of forward to with interest
' good wishes to you.

Sincerely

Gilbert Watson

RONNIE CORBETT

Two distinct features of this writing are the smallness of the small letters and the wide spacing between the words and lines.

The smallness of the letters shows that the writer is quite brainy; has an excellent mind that can concentrate on details; and can sum-up situations quickly and correctly. Judgement is good and there is a highly developed critical sense.

The neat wide spacing of the letters shows ability to organise personal details. There is care in choosing friends and firmly-rooted ideas and convictions. Luxuries of life are enjoyed and there is interest in cultural subjects.

Shape of the letters indicates moderate aggressiveness and connection of the letters confirms reliable and painstaking qualities. Occasional breaks in the connections indicate flashes of intuition.

The tendency of finals to dip to the right shows some obstinacy and flashes of temper.

Long lower loops indicate considerable virility and a down-to-earth nature. High placing of the i dots directly above the stem shows a precise and exact nature. It also indicates every endeavour is made to be a perfectionist.

The fairly short t crosses indicate a desire to feel settled and a dislike of changing habits.

Firmness of the t crosses shows a determination of purpose, self-assurance and will-power.

storious . and illegible

I hope you "make" more of

Have a wonderful New Year .

You . Bruce Corett

This is a perfect example of symbolic writing when a person illustrates the greatest interests.

In this sample all the capital letters are like musical symbols and show interest and preoccupation in music.

Long initial loops to the words show a tendency to procrastinate and time is taken before the writer's mind is made up.

Size of the capital letters in relation to the middle zone shows self-confidence and the shape of the letters m shows that strong opinions are held and there is no fear of expressing these.

The long finals indicate generosity and the fact that the writer deliberately chose to write this message with a strong upward slant indicates general optimism and a hard-to-discourage quality.

My dear Frazer

I do know what of an make of this: —

Yours truly

WENDY CRAIG

The level base line in combination with the evenness of the letters and the closed letters a and o show a loyalty to friends, a sincere nature and an ability to know when to keep silent.

Upright slope of the writing shows shrewd thinking and writing abilities. Normally the writer is not easily fooled, but the exaggerated bases of capital letters show a degree of credulity.

Size emphasis on the middle zone of small letters shows a predominant interest in what is happening in the present.

Layout of the specimen, which is in the form of a poem instead of a letter, suggests that the writer is paying more attention to style and neatness than would be normal. However it is clear the writer has a tidy mind, is an excellent judge of character, has a charitable outlook toward people, and enjoys the good things in life.

Arched formation of the small letters indicate that though outwardly informal in manner the writer really is quite reserved and is perfectly happy to enjoy their own company and thoughts.

Initial letters without a loop show fixed ideas of an original thinker. The placing of the i dots shows intuition and an ability to act on it. The t crosses show energy, enthusiasm and imagination.

Bottomley.
  1874 - 1948.

..n destroy a blade
   of grass
on England at
   her roots:
..r no man's foot
   can pass
evermore no ....
   life shoots

Like myself this writer is left-handed. The writing is extremely small with a slight leftward tendency.

The very small writing shows above-average intelligence.

Neat layout and spacing combined with the dotting of the letters i directly above the stem indicate an ability to work out things carefully and powers of concentration, which is quite common with left-handed writers. (The process of learning to write a natural script designed for right-handed writers is tiring to the hand and mind and requires extra powers of concentration at any early age.)

Short t crosses to the right show plenty of energy, a lively nature and an enthusiasm about work.

The size of the signature, which is exactly the same as the body of the letter, shows lack of ostentation and modesty.

The cheeky bulbous lower loops show physical stamina and coy virility.

PETER CUSHING

The two most noticeable features of this specimen are the extremely small size of the middle zone of writing and the wide spacing between words and lines.

The small size of the writing shows intelligence well above average and an excellent memory. Great attention is paid to details and situations are judged quickly and accurately.

Wide spacing between words and lines shows a neat and orderly mind. Affairs are organised well. There also is excellent judgement of character and fair dealings with others.

The spacing also indicates a degree of extravagance and enjoyment of the luxuries of life. This type of writer is usually interested in cultural subjects: may be a patron of the arts; and most likely has a hobby which is taken very seriously.

Width of the left margin emphasises an aesthetic and cultural outlook.

Pressure of the writing is strong and certain letters are filled in and the lower loops are long.

Apart from giving indications of strong sexual and physical strength, it seems that the cultural interests and hobbies may be devoted to rather robust fields.

Extension of the writing show spontaneity and the ability to be a good mixer and a learned conversationalist. Delays are disliked.

The short finals and the closed letters a and o show an occasional desire to retire from the limelight to enjoy being alone with own thoughts.

There is discretion and a knowledge of when to keep secrets.

Disconnection of the letters within words shows a creative, imaginative and intuitive mind and most of the bright ideas work out well.

be blinded by their tears, or the

" treasure awaits the in the

" Death. My friend - will give

[signature]

DAVID DIMBLEBY

Slope of this writing is perpendicular with a slight leftward tendency. In conjunction with the style of writing this indicates that the subject has a rather cool and analytical outlook toward people and what is going on in the world.

General appearance of the writing and the simple unadorned capital I indicate that, apart from having a basically distrusting nature, the writer may well be own harshest critic.

There is natural interest in literature and cultured subjects. In creative work there is not a lot of ideas. Instead, things are worked out carefully and logically and there is a liking to be neat, precise and accurate.

Lower loops hooking to the right instead of the left indicate aggressiveness. The shape of the i dots indicate a natural sense of wit and humour.

The tightly closed letters a and o show an inbred secretiveness and an ability to conceal true thoughts.

Shape of the t crosses shows bursts of energy and enthusiasm. They also confirm an active ferreting mind.

lways been suspicious
of tests because I bel-
ieve it to contain a hard
but this, I assume, is
an illiterate, genuine
revealing scrawl.

Yours sincerely

David Kimberley

DIANA DORS

The wide swooping lower y loops which look rather like inverted capital letters d, show strong sexual ability, interest in other physical sports, and a good down-to-earth character.

The writing tends to change slopes, which indicates moodiness at times. There is level-headed sense and keen judgement.

Even spacing between the lines shows thinking ability with an inclination to be somewhat extroverted.

The narrow left margin shows the practical side of the writer's nature, although the long finals and extension of letters show the kindness and generosity of someone who can be a bit of a spendthrift and almost certainly likes a gamble.

Evenness of the letters show a painstaking and conscientious quality.

The tightly closed letters a and o show an ability to be diplomatic and a knowledge of when to keep a secret.

Height of the capital letters shows self-respect, self-confidence and pride.

A sensitive side to nature perhaps indicates a poetic interest and an enjoyment of flattery.

Placing of the i dots and the t crosses show a changeable side of nature.

The i dots to the left show a tendency to put off doing things until the last moment, but the long t crosses indicate that at other times quick decisions are made and there is apt to be a rush to get things done quickly.

The down-sloping t crosses show stubbornness and obstinacy.

The shape of the small letters n and w show a good ability to adapt to the vicissitudes of life.

Sir twice to you, + if I do this
you will read something mysterious
out about us in Monday morning.
So here it is + lets I hope you
can decipher it.

Sincerely yours,

BRUCE FORSYTH

This very interesting specimen shows the verve and vigour of the writer.

The upward slope of the horizontal line of the writing shows the optimism of a live-wire go-getter who would máke a good salesman.

However, like most subjects with this temperament there is evidence of rather quick changes of moods. This is shown by the variations in slants of the letters.

Predominant rightward trend of the writing with the urgency to get to the right hand of the page shows general buoyancy and interest in what is going to happen next.

The few but sudden leftward tendencies indicate a tendency to take a second look before leaping.

Generous spacing of the writing and the high capitals and strong style show adequate self-confidence and some extrovertness.

Extension of the letters show a chatty type who can mix well and be good entertainer.

Evenness of the small letters shows the writer is reliable and painstaking at work.

The closed letters a and o show an ability to be secretive when needed.

Disconnection of letters within words is another dominant feature and this shows the writer to be creative and full of ideas. These are arrived at hastily and intuitively and some are wrong but most are right.

Witty and quick on the trigger, the writer has an ability to weigh up a situation almost instantly.

Likes and dislikes are liable to be formed at first sight, and the writer is difficult to deceive.

waiting for the
d Breath to the.

on Soon.

JUDY GEESON

Dominant feature of this writing is the sharp angular formation of the letters. This signifies a real live-wire, both physically and mentally. Schemes are thought up and seen through.

Letter connection confirms a quick and logical mind.

This writer can be argumentative and once the mind is made up it is difficult to change it.

There is strong artistic and creative ability.

The absent finals show the practical side of nature.

Shape of the capitals show the writer likes to get down to brass tacks.

The i dots to the right indicate some impulsiveness.

Shape of t crosses shows determination and healthy desire for self-improvement.

PS Nei to all you again on what on how to speak.

Unely Burn.

LARRY GRAYSON

The individual letters of this message look as though they are being blown about by the wind.

Individual letters almost always being disconnected show nervous excitable energy. (Bruce Forsyth's handwriting is very similar.)

This writing of a person full of ideas, who never stays still and who always acts on impulses and intuition.

The i dots are high and to the right. The dots in the form of dashes confirm insatiable curiosity and an inability to let the mind rest. These also are the sign of natural wit and humour.

es Trases

How very nice to
on Pete Murray's
this morning
I always enjoy t
programme

There is a dominance of the upper zone in this writing which shows a strong interest in the more pleasant sides of life. There is a tendency to clutch for these and be a bit of a daydreamer.

Extremely small size of the middle zone shows an excellent and logical mind. There is concentration on details and a grasping of situations correctly.

Power of the lower zone shows physical strength and ability.

Hooked t crosses show tenacity. However the fact that these are nearly always to the left shows a tendency to procrastinate and there may be quite a few occasions when time is taken for the mind to be made up.

Dashing shape of the i dots shows energy and enthusiasm. The writer also is witty and has a natural sense of humour.

that their life will be fu
may be worth your effort i
nament — Nothing is bette
ach manent can be fallen to
t viewpoint . Stay on

Best

Jy Hardin

A straightforward nature is shown by the horizontal evenness of the word lines and in conjunction with the even, individual letters honesty is confirmed.

Slight horizontal rising of the lines to the right of the page indicates the writer is of an optimistic nature. And the rightward, vertical slope of the individual letter reveals self-control.

Wide spacing between the words and lines shows an excellent judge of character and good organising ability.

The rounded letters m and n show a dislike of violence.

The extended flow of the words indicate courage and daring.

Tops of the letters a and o sometimes are closed and sometimes open. This shows that the writer believes in calling a spade a spade.

Letters of the words nearly always are connected, showing prudency and practicality.

High capital letters show a healthy self-respect.

Long downstrokes mean a love of outdoor sports and physical strength.

Triangular downstrokes of the letters y shows a strongly materialistic and, at times, domineering nature.

The dash dots over the letters i show plenty of energy, enthusiasm and a witty sense of humour.

Short t crosses indicate caution at the right time.

If my handouts
hope it is for
and naturally
alteration in
hope this is

good.

SIR ROBERT HELPMANN

This is one of the best graphological specimens I have received. It epitomises the character of the writer. It is a perfect example of writing that shows the writer to be in the right job.

Long sweeping lower loops show considerable physical strength and a high degree of sensuality.

Upper loops show the strong cultural sense of an idealist.

Letter connection shows logical reasoning full of intuition. There is an abundance of creative ideas, most of which are followed through.

The distinct leftward tendency indicates a person not particularly easy to mix with—in fact (by the combination with the size of letters) rather difficult at times. There is an extravagant temperament and a rather hot temper.

Behind the love for grandeur and display there is a strong and determined nature. Also loyalty and generosity to friends.

The very low dotting of the letter i show precision and accuracy. Hooks in the t crosses show tenacity, which confirms the determination of nature.

It is a great pleasure to be on "The Pete Murray Show". I hope the London Season of the Australian Ballet will be a success. It is a good young Company

Robert Helpmann

JIMMY HILL

Broad shaded writing shows an insistent nature and quite a distinctive personality with a materialistic and sensuous nature.

There is strong will, perseverance, diligence and a degree of severity with considerable self-confidence and situations tend to be dominated.

This strong writing also displays natural interest in outdoor sports and an especial interest where physical strength and skill is required.

Shape of letters y indicates a degree of selfishness and self-interest.

Shape of the capital I, sweeping from the left, indicates rebelliousness.

A clear, logical and enquiring mind is indicated and spacing of the letter and the writing shows a good organiser.

Crossing of the 't to the right shows enthusiasm, energy and liveliness.

Murray,

I think you's

the best on the radio & I re
to listen to it!'

Your fan.

Jimmy Gill.

only you would allow yo
rpnt a decent team, such i
Coventry you'd be well nigh

GORDON JACKSON

Instead of a specimen of natural handwriting I have been given this sample of calligraphy by Gordon Jackson.

Calligraphic handwriting is when the subject deliberately renounces the school-taught style of writing and decides to write in a meticulous and ornate manner.

From a graphologist's point of view this makes it very difficult to judge the true character of the subject since there is a double meaning to the switch from normal handwriting to calligraphy.

Either the writer had or has an inferiority complex and is making a determined attempt to assert character in a world he believes is against him, or the subject has a naturally artistic or flamboyant nature and adopts this style to reinforce his appearance.

I would say Gordon Jackson falls into the first category.

There probably was a time when he felt he was not sufficiently projecting himself. He has a natural shy and reticent nature which is not always an asset in show business.

He made a determined and obviously successful effort to overcome this.

Anyone who adopts this style of handwriting has a natural artistic nature and an interest in form and beauty.

'This is an example
writing!
Queen Elizabeth
ce!

Gordan Jackson

DANNY LA RUE

Dominant feature of this writing is the size, combined with a strong rightward slant and sweeping lower loops.

These factors in combination with the sharpness of the letter formation show the writer has:

A good state of health and mind and has boundless energy.

A mind that is keen and creative.

Not a particulary warm nature.

The hooks on the t crosses show determination, tenacity and will-power. Although there may be an explosive temper grudges are not likely to be borne.

The sweeping and strong lower loops confirm down-to-earth nature, stamina and sensual voluptuousness.

CHRISTOPHER LEE

The strong fast flowing style of this writing mirrors the confidence and self-assurance of the writer.

A noticeable feature is that not only are the letters within the words connected but also the words are frequently connected.

This shows a person not to be trifled with. A stickler for principles who cannot be shaken from fixed and decided ideas. In pursuit of these there is stubborness and obstinacy.

Because of conservative outlook the writer is unlikely to go in for trendy clothes or pursuits.

Probably a dim view is taken of the permissive society.

High capital letters, particularly the letter I, which are the ego symbols, confirm self-assurance, self-confidence and pride in achievements.

Perpendicular slant indicates a certain aloofness, a keen analytical mind with excellent critical ability and good sound judgement.

The narrow left margin emphasises a practical outlook and the narrow right margin shows keen interest in life, people and the future.

Very heavy pressure of the writing shows a sensual and materialistic person who enjoys good food and the physical pleasures of life. There is an interest in sport, particularly when physical skill and strength is involved.

The separated downstrokes of the small letters d shows a quiet nature with a tendency to be taciturn at times.

The heavy dots above the small letters i show a strong will and materialistic nature.

Dash-shaped i dots shows enthusiasm and energy. Although at times the writer becomes irritable and is inclined to worry.

A noticeable feature of the writing is that the t crosses are turned down at the right. This indicates a good repartee and some sarcasm.

I have never ha
analysis made by a
such as yourself — a
always interested me

It seems amazi
be possible to "read" a
writing — but it has be
proved in many cases.
interested to receive yo

Sincerely

Ch——

LIBERACE

This is an excellent example of symbolic handwriting, though of course it is not natural. It is simulated deliberately to project the character and profession of the writer. No average person automatically would draw the image of something like a piano as part of the normal signature.

He obviously knows that to make your mark in life you have to fight for yourself, but this has not blunted his generosity.

The extension of the writing and the long finals show he is extravagantly generous.

The curved hook back on the finals show that he is protective.

However he also protects those near and dear to him and he is a good friend to have.

Equally he could be a bitter enemy to people who upset him or his friends. He could be termed possessively loyal.

The pronounced upward slant of the lines shows he is a born optimist, and it would take a great deal to knock him off his piano stool.

To Fraser,
It's lonely to be
back in London to
introduce my new
Auto-biography,

Liberace

Nov. 30th — 1923

This is a perfect writing specimen of a person who is full of energy, both mentally and physically.

Speed of writing, letter connection and the joining of one word to another shows this intense mental energy. There is stubborness and obstinacy, decided opinions and a stickler for principles. Likely to be conservative in both manner and dress. Sweeping lower loops show considerable physical strength and good health.

Although not immodest, there is self-confidence and the ability to size-up a situation quickly and correctly. If called upon there is the ability to take charge of a situation without any fuss.

Shape of the letters d and simplification of the word "of" shows strong cultural interests and an intellectual mind.

The i dots are in two forms. One is a sweeping stroke which shows intense enthusiasm; and the other is a semi-circle, which shows intense curiosity and an inquiring mind. Enjoys meeting people and observing them. These observations become a filing system in the writer's mind. Perhaps likely to have a sharp and rather an explosive temper which dies down quickly. Not a person to bear grudges.

I am glad
his show I
... ...
an old admirer

VIRGINIA McKENNA

This is strong healthy rightward sloping handwriting. It shows the friendly nature of an outgoing person who takes a keen interest in personal projects and enjoys meeting people.

Narrowness of letters indicates a practical nature with appreciation of things being neat and tidy.

The dashing t crosses indicate enthusiasm. The writer likes to get schemes done as quickly as possible and there might be some impatience.

Shape of the letters indicates cultural interests which are most likely to be in the field of literature.

There is plenty of imagination and writing ability.

o sorry to have
it; but I was
minutes in the
Thank goodness
in time. It wl
e Pete Murray aga
rs,

Virginia McKenna

There is a strong rightward slope to the letters; the horizontal lines are slanting upwards and the high flowing upper loops are a dominant feature of the writing.

The rightward slope shows an amicable and friendly person, not given to airs and graces. Being fully aware and proud of achievements is shown by the large capital letters I and M.

In particular the flying initial loop of the M shows strong opinions and a firm determination to see them through.

The upward sloping t crosses show this is not the type to sit back.

There is a continuing effort for self-improvement. The hooks at the end of the t crosses show tenacity.

The i dots and the shape of the g indicate a good sense of humour and a conversationalist. The upper loops indicate an idealist.

The knotted letters f, a and o indicate a sense of being secretive when needed.

here this morni

! too early ā I'm t

t you'll find yo

[signature]

Rounded form of the letter bases show the writer nearly always is peace-loving, good natured and tries to avoid all arguments and fights.

However, combination of the extension of writing and formation of certain individual letters, including the loop on the upper stem of the letters d, shows that emotion can take over and be expressed in strong forceful language, becoming rather demonstrative in the process.

Extended form of the writing shows the spontaneity, initiative, courage and daring of a good mixer, a good talker and entertainer.

Signs show the writer could be a bit of a spendthrift and perhaps likes to have a gamble.

Long finals show the writer to be generous, liberal and considerate of the feelings of others.

Letter connection shows a logical mind.

Initial downstrokes without loops show originality.

There is quite a distinctive personality with fixed opinions and set ideas.

The looped letters d show sensitivity and susceptibility to flattery.

The left looped letters f shows a quick mind.

Continuously connected letters show a very logical mind which takes great care for important decisions.

Shape of the small letters w and n show an ability to adapt to circumstances.

conference (the

v players bore

four weeks t

would be t

v demanding t

[signature]

Dominant style of this writing is the arcade formation, although the secondary style is the sharp letter formation.

The arcade part of the writer is where there are two characters.

Mixing with people and being a conversationalist is one part but there are occasions when the subject wants to get away from people and enjoy the solitude of own thoughts and appreciate nature rather than people.

Although arcade writers may appear to be free and easy, they are usually not. They tend to be tensed up inwardly. They are difficult to get to know really well.

Sharp letter formations in this writing show the strong creative side the writer has and the strong powers of observation. This active inquiring mind is doubly emphasised by the sharp shape of the i dots.

The staccato style of the writing confirms the subject has an abundance of nervous energy—not the type of person to remain still for long whether in speech or action.

Shape of the letters b, h, and f denotes culture and good taste.

Shape of the t crosses indicate a quick temper but the temper dies down rapidly.

Although the layout of the letter shows a precise neat and tidy mind, there obviously are times of forgetfulness.

ers of Gatley, Cheshire:

three years for replies

no. Yesterday he got a

£40,000 in an Irish

best of British luck to

-la, a fol-de-lay, and

iss

Patrick Moore

STIRLING MOSS

Dominant features of this writing are the smallness of letters, the lightness of pressure and the wide spacing between words and lines.

Smallness of letters shows that the writer has an above-average mind and can concentrate on details with fine judgement and keen perception.

Pressure of the writing shows refinement. In private life tastes and manners are quiet and unassuming.

Wide spacing between words and lines shows a good organiser who can manage business affairs well. There are firmly-rooted ideas and convictions. Also an interest in cultural subjects.

The narrow left margin emphasises a nature with a practical side.

Evenness of the small letters show pains to be reliable and painstakingly conscientious.

Short finals indicate reticence and not an easy mixer.

Shape of the letters a and o show frankness and sincerity.

Left-looping of letters f shows fluency of thought and a quick mind.

The i dots high and to the right indicate an eagerness to find out about things.

Shape of the i dots indicate enthusiasm and energy. There also are moods of irritability with an inclination to worry at times.

Dear Mr White,

As promised I am writing a short note to confirm that I should be at 489 3272 or 7962 from 10.00 am onwards on monday June 19th. If you cannot read this, please call for a translation.

PETE MURRAY

What a rough and untidy specimen this is—but at least it is natural! I am referring to the handwriting of course.

The speed of the writing and the strong rightward slope indicates a quick and lively mind which is often ahead of the actual actions of the owner.

Spacing of the words and between the lines shows only moderate organising ability.

Frequent omission of the i dots indicates absent-mindedness. When the i dots do appear they indicate wit and humour.

Wide-open letters a and o indicate some inability to keep secrets.

Upward slope of the lines shows energy, optimism and determination. Not easily discouraged.

Left looping of the letters f confirms quick thinking and fluency of thoughts.

Finals are long, but curl back, which indicates stubbornness and tenacity. Friendly in a courteous way, the writer also can be tactless and outspoken.

Shape of the lower loops indicates that sexually he has reached the simmering-down stage.

Fraser,

the time comes

Scotch Whisky is
ol. to be Advertised
'/ Shall reccomen
an excellent Reser
celving.!!

Good luck

Your Soti Friend

Pete Murray

The urgent pace of this letter shows a mind brimming with energy and imaginative thinking.

This is vividly revealed by the connection of the letters and the style of certain individual small letters.

Quick-flowing connection of letters indicates creativity.

The occasional breaks between the letters in words reveal an intuitive nature.

Inclined to reach decisions instinctively and hastily. The writer sizes up situations quickly. Likes and dislikes are usually formed on first impressions and he is difficult to deceive.

The t crosses are high on the stem, confirming imagination and creative ability. Tendency to get very excited about new projects and ideas and perhaps irritable if others do not share enthusiasm.

The t crosses to the right show energy, liveliness and enthusiasm.

Shortness of the t crosses shows that ways or habits are not wished to be changed.

The i dots high to the right show curiosity and the dash shape of the dots confirms enthusiastic and lively nature.

Height of upper loops in letters h and l shows imaginative mind and interest in new ideas.

Height of capital letters shows self-respect, self-confidence and pride.

Small letters a and o are not always closed at the top, which indicates frankness and truthfulness.

Final strokes of letters e descend strongly to the right showing temper and obstinacy.

Unevenness of the small letter within the words and variations in slope of letters confirms a restless and changeable nature.

Size and width of writing shows spontaneous wit that stands well as a good mixer and entertainer. Inclined to take a gamble and possibly overspend at times. Also inclined to be impatient.

General wide spacing between words and lines shows firmly-rooted ideas and convictions. Enjoys the best things in life and is interested in the arts and cultural subjects.

To Fraser —
      with this
b —— g ball point
I hardly dare say
how much I
admire your art.

      . Yours ever

      [signature]

      —·—

MARJORIE PROOPS

The quick urgency of the writing shown by the linking of words without a break plus the linking of the i dots to the opening letter of the next word demonstrates why she is at the top of her profession. She is tough and has to be, because she is a woman in what used to be a man's world.

She has an urgent sense to get on with things.

She is stubborn and obstinate. When she makes up her mind it will take a tractor engine to make her change it.

She is a stickler for principles.

The flowing form of the writing shows distinct creative ability.

She likes to live in pleasant and luxurious surroundings, but budgets carefully to achieve this since she has a practical nature.

High capitals show full confidence in herself and her decisions.

Lower loops are either straight down without a loop showing her down-to-earthness, or are looped to the left showing a quick and fluent mind.

Long t strokes indicate she makes quick decisions and likes to carry them out in a speedy manner.

Uncramped style of the writing shows spontaneity. She can think up good ideas and is a good mixer and talker.

The tendency for words to taper down in size shows that she can drive a hard bargain. She is extremely shrewd, discreet, diplomatic and subtle.

Final strokes of certain and letters descending below the line confirm her obstinacy and a tendency to have strong prejudices.

And here's hoping

have a very

careful trip

.

Stuart,
Major

CLIFF RICHARD

I last analysed this handwriting 15 years ago and it is interesting to note that the basic features remain the same. The marked difference is the tremendous increase in confidence.

There is an upward slant to the lines showing that his optimistic nature has been retained.

As before, the dominance of the handwriting is still in the upper zone which shows strong spiritual interests, idealism and a tendency to daydream at times.

The left margin and narrow right margin show a strong desire to communicate with and meet people.

Shape of the lower loops indicate that private life is restricted to a close circle of friends to whom there is loyalty.

The i dots are still directly above the stem and low, showing care applied to work.

Low placing of the t crosses indicates genuine modesty.

Size of the capitals shows considerable pride in personal achievements.

Tendency of the upper loops to bend slightly forward confirm modesty and show a degree of humility.

anks for asking me
show! Hope all is
that you have a fa
= an amazing New Y

Cliff Richard

HARRY SECOMBE

This specimen is of very natural handwriting which shows that the subject behaves naturally and without ostentation in both public and private life.

He is peace-loving and good-natured and dislikes getting involved in arguments or physical violence.

He has a liking for the best in music and other cultural subjects and has creative ability in these fields.

Extension of the letters shows a good mixer, a good teller of stories, and life and soul of the party. He does this not so much like to satisfy his own ego as to make other people happy.

The almost total lack of margin to the left of the page shows he is extremely prudent in personal affairs.

Long finals show an extreme generosity to others.

Shape of certain letters and words show that his ability to keep secrets when necessary and he can be quite diplomatic when need be. He may avoid telling the truth if he feels it will hurt the person concerned.

The height of the capital letters shows that he has an adequate measure of self-confidence and self-respect.

Dominant feature of the individual letters is the left looping of letters f, which reveals a quick mind and fluency of thought.

The low crossing of the bars of the letters t shows a degree of humility.

Wuts

  Jhr is a special
d. writing, which, if you
perhaps you will take
to chemist, and he'l
re prescription for you.

  Sincerely

  Harry L Coutts

BILL SIMPSON

The high upper zone shows an idealist who has a strong sense of the spiritual values of life.

The sharp i dashes show a natural sense of wit and humour but the dominant placing of them directly above the stem indicates precision and accuracy in the work undertaken.

Shape of the t crosses indicates temper is likely to be quick, but it dies down equally quickly.

Wide left margin and narrow right margin indicate confidence grows as he warms to his subject. Observant of people and world happenings.

The closed letters a and o indicate he is not much of a gossip and knows when to keep confidences.

Fraser,

How nice of you to
come to the Beeb.
such a cold morning
we'll warm up.
you can organize
the coffee

JOHN TREVELYAN

This interesting specimen of handwriting is neatly spaced on the page.

Size of the writing is extremely small with a perfect balance between the upper, middle and lower zones.

Letter slant is almost perpendicular and the letter formation shows natural simplification.

All this shows that we have a writer with an extremely active and incisive mind who is a natural organiser and executive. Able to sum-up situations quickly, calmly and efficiently. Not the type to get into a panic.

Complete absence of initial strokes shows he is not the type to procrastinate. When he wants to do something or get things done, he succeeds.

Firm downstrokes with a tendency to hook to the right shows a down-to-earth attitude and a degree of aggressiveness.

Firm t crossing and the decided down-slant show strong opinions and impatience with people who disagree.

Dashes of letters i to the right show a natural curiosity and enquiring mind. Shape of them shows an excellent sense of wit and humour.

now quite Early in the morning
or in retirement I can choose

However I quite enjoy coming House. In the _last_ two or here several times since last time was published, and people talk about it

pleasure to meet you here.

With good wishes

Yours sincerely

John Trevelyan

FRANKIE VAUGHAN

This is fast flowing writing with a pronounced rightward slope. There is very light pressure in the writing.

This indicates the energy and restrained exhuberance of the writer.

Lightness of the pressure indicates a basically gentle nature with a dislike of violence.

Long dashing t crosses indicate a rather impulsive nature with a desire to get things done quickly.

Size of the capitals and their shape indicates no lack of self-confidence.

The i dots directly above the stem indicates precision and accuracy, although he works hard and carefully to achieve the air of relaxation.

Slope of the writing, flow and curve of the lower loops show athletic ability and considerable grace of movement.

High crossing of the letters t shows an imaginative mind, and in combination with the shape of letters creative abilities are revealed.

Long hooked initial loops indicate a lively nature and a tendency to be a bit of a chatterer.

This is only a short specimen but its gentle even flow well reflects the personality of the writer. It shows natural artistry and an ease of presentation.

The strong healthy rightward slope shows a calm but enthusiastic outlook toward life and people.

Long finals show a generous nature.

Emphasis on the middle zone indicates a pre-occupation with the present with a liking to take things as they come.

Strong but gentle lower loops indicate physical strength and warmth.

Connection of letters within the words without any breaks indicate the writer likes to reason things out calmly rather than making rush decisions.

Shape of the capital letter "M" in particular shows the writer can hold strong opinions and is not afraid to air them.

Dear Marshall

Hope you are well

All my love

Dad

Vaughan

VIRGINIA WADE

The widening left margin shows that she braces herself for the task ahead and becomes increasingly confident as she proceeds.

Although she is keenly interested in people and affairs, her character in writing shows restraint and indicates she is not likely to be gushing or over-effusive.

Shape of the letters shows obvious cultural interests and artistic appreciation.

In particular the graceful curves of the lower loops reveals physical grace.

Shape of the capital letters I and the low crossing of the letters t shows restraint and quite a degree of modesty and dignity.

The i dots to the right show an enquiring and observant mind with a quiet sense of humour and wit.

Basically this is a logical thinker but she gets the odd flashes of intuition and is not afraid to act on them.

The shape of the letters r shows energy and enthusiasm.

. It's much too early &
morning to collect any int
thoughts together — but by
I've heard a few more live
records I might be in .

form

Virginia

MISS WORLD (MARJORIE WALLACE)

This is a specimen of very symbolic handwriting.

The capital I looks more like a capital O.

This wide right looped I indicates that the subject carries all before her.

Lower loops are equally eye-catching. They are long, low and gracefully inflated.

This indicates quite a down-to-earth nature, physical grace and sensual energy.

Excellent form of the writing shows clearly that the subject is certainly not a case of all beauty and no brains.

It reveals considerable intelligence and a logical and creative mind. She is likely to have a natural sense of colour and design.

The shape of the g and e indicates an interest in cultural subjects.

The very long finals and the extension of the letters indicate a naturally friendly and generous nature. They also indicate a degree of extravagance.

Shape of the t crosses show energy and enthusiasm, while the hooks on them indicate determination and tenacity.

Fraser—

I so glad to be

am anxious to see,

o say in analysis

riting. I'm aba

, so I'd better

Bye

The obvious features of this subject's handwriting are the extreme smallness of the writing, the speed and the fineness.

Extreme smallness shows it is writing of an intellectual with ability of extreme concentration.

The vertical slope shows strong head control, an analytical mind and sharp judgement.

He has great creative ability and as is confirmed by the left looping of the letters f he has a quick and fertile mind.

The even spacing between lines and words shows an excellent organising ability. He has a fine sense of justice and is a good judge of character. Firmly rooted ideas and convictions.

The fineness of the writing shows that in private life his tastes are simple and that he has an unassuming character.

Evenness of the small letters shows that he is painstaking and conscientious.

Short or absent finals show that he is prudent and self-reliant. He is not naturally the "life and soul of the party".

Downstrokes made without a loop confirm that he has originality of thought, fixed opinions and set ideas.

Low stem of the letters d shows shrewdness.

Upstroke of the stem of letters such as p and q shows aggressiveness and a definite tendency to be sarcastic.

Dots to the right on the small letters i, confirmed by the break in letters within words, show that at times the subject can be impulsive and act on intuition.

A strong feature is the dash formation of the dots above the letters i, which shows that the subject is full of enthusiasm and energy. But he has moods of irritability.

The distinct tendency of the t crosses to slope downwards shows that he can be stubborn and obstinate.

of engineering, particularly chemical engineering.

In July I expressed the anxiety of [...] about the dangers of a [...] failing — if [...] entry stage — through difficulties with [...] conduct course students. [...] more [...]-sponsoring students. This seems to be more an anxiety [...] to believe than a current problem, but nothing Park has happened since on list. Corporation has in any way diminished it.

151

This strong handwriting shows considerable energy, strength of character and determination.

The perpendicular slope of the writing shows an analytical mind with good reasoning powers, keen judgement and good emotional control.

Regular spacing confirms these points and emphasises considerable self-confidence.

A dominant feature is thickness of the writing, tendency for certain letters to be filled in and the inflated lower loops, which shows the strong virility of the subject. He enjoys the sports and physical pleasures of life.

Extension shows ability to be a good mixer, a good teller of stories and an entertainer.

Evenness of the letters shows the care taken in work.

Shortness of the finals in combination with the slope of letters indicates that in private life he can be rather reticent and retiring.

The closed letters a and o show that he is tactful, diplomatic and well able to keep secrets.

Connected letters again confirm the practical side of his nature. He likes to take time to think things out and never makes up his mind hastily on matters of importance.

Placing of the letters i dots directly above the stem shows precision; the dots to the right show curiosity and powers of observation.

Long vigorous t crosses show a desire to get things done quickly.

Upward slope of the crosses shows plenty of healthy ambition.

— If you havent had
my Cabaret dates by
— Now. let me.
let you. leave them.
sign.
Kindest Regards.
Mike

STARS IN THIS BOOK HAVE BEEN SELECTED FROM
THIS ABRIDGED LIST OF CELEBRITIES WHOSE
WRITING HAS BEEN ANALYSED BY FRASER WHITE
In alphabetical order

John Alderton
Terrence Alexander
Barry Alldis
Malcolm Allison
Lord Arran
Richard Attenborough
Max Audley
Long John Baldry
David Bailey
Gordon Banks
Ray Barnett
The Beatles
Jeff Beck
Cilla Black
Tony Blackburn
Daniel Boone
Pat Boone
Tony Britton
Faith Brook
Max Bygraves
Phyllis Calvert
Violet Carsons
Roy Castle
Johnny Cash
Bobby Charlton
Jackie Charlton
Ralph Coates
Les Cocker
Michael Codron
Perry Como
Adrienne Corri
Ronnie Corbett
Kenneth Cope

Des Champ
George Cooper
Wendy Craig
Michael Crawford
Bernard Cribbins
Michael Croft
Peter Cushing
Paul Daneman
Rupert Davies
John Christian Dee
Terry Dene
Michael Dennison
David Dimbleby
Ken Dodd
Val Doonican
Donovan
Robert Dougall
Diana Dors
Terry Downes
Pete Drummond
John Dunn
Jimmy Edwards
Denholm Elliot
Dick Emery
Kenny Everett
The Everly Brothers
Gerald Flood
Clinton Ford
John Finch
Bruce Forsyth
Barry Foster
Leo Franklyn
Princess Galitzine

Judy Geeson
Deborah Grant
Jill Gray
Johnny Gray
Joan Greenwood
Robin Hall
Kenneth Haig
Ty Hardin
George Harrison
Sir Robert Helpmann
David Hemmings
Dickie Henderson
Marie Herbert
Joan Hickson
Graham Hill
Vince Hill
Mary Holland
Sally Anne Howes
Emlyn Hughes
Barry Humphries
Gayle Hunnicut
Woody Herman
Sheila Hancock
Roy Hyde
Mick Jagger
Tom Jones
Janis Joplin
Syd James
Gordon Jackson
Derek Jewell
Jean Kent
Brian Labone
Danny La Rue
Christopher Lee
John Lennon
Tommy Leonetti
Liberace
Margaret Lockwood
David Lodge
Lulu
Joanna Lumley
Jack de Manio
Alfred Marks

Johnny Mathis
Ronald Maxwell
Virginia McKenna
John Mills
Bobby Moore
Patrick Moore
Matt Monro
Johnny Moran
Stirling Moss
Alan Mullery
Paul McCartney
Chas McDevitt
Kenneth McKellar
Rod McKuen
Jimmy McGregor
Bob McNab
Robert Nesbitt
David Niven
Johnny Nash
Des O'Connor
Julian Orchard
Nicholas Parsons
John Peel
Donald Peers
Jon Pertwee
Leslie Phillips
Pat Phoenix
Gene Pitney
Margaret Powell
Elvis Presley
Marjorie Proops
P. J. Proby
Raymonde (Teasie-Weasie)
Robin Ray
Ralph Reader
Beryl Reid
Toby Robertson
James Robertson-Justice
Cliff Richard
Johnny Ray
Mike Raven
Les Reed
Brian Rix

Rachel Roberts
Anne Rogers
Emperor Rosko
Rev. Fred Secombe
Harry Secombe
Peter Sellers
David Sadler
Terry Scott
Peter Shilton
Harold Shepherdson
Don Short
Bill Simpson
John Snagge
Terry Spinks
Ringo Starr
John Stride
Jacqueline Susanne
Eric Sykes
Jimmy Tarbuck
Peter Thompson
Anne Todd
Dave Lee Travis

Bill Travers
John Trevelyan
Frankie Vaughan
Norman Vaughan
Sarah Vaughan
Virginia Wade
Max Wall
Jack Watling
Elizabeth Welch
Carl Wayne
Emlyn Williams
Kenneth Williams
Paul Williams
Rt Hon. Harold Wilson
Barbara Windsor
Edward Woodward
Bruce Wyndham
Mike Watts
Mike Yarwood
Susannah York
Jimmy Young

WHAT THE CELEBRITIES SAY . . .

Terence Alexander—"Absolutely marvellous—it's so right."

Lord Arran—"Well I have all those qualities. I think it is a pretty accurate analysis."

Richard Attenborough—"How can he be so monstrously accurate?"

David Bailey—"It's all true. I quite like this handwriting business."

Gordon Banks—"That's very very true—I think he's gorgeous!"

Ian Bannen—"Very true."

Cilla Black—"He's good is Fraser White—he's smashing!"

Tony Blackburn—"It's fantastic. He's come up with a real winner."

Daniel Boone—"He's a very lucky man. I'm afraid he's right."

Pat Boone—"Dead correct. That is the story of my life."

Faith Brook—"I'm amazed; he has got me in a nutshell."

Max Bygraves—"I think he has hit the nail right on the head. I am a great believer in this handwriting analysis."

Phyllis Calvert—"He is absolutely right."

Glen Campbell—"Amazing, amazing."

Violet Carson—"Fraser White is astonishingly right. He's good."

Judy Geeson—"It's all very true."

Jackie Charlton—"I agree with everything he says."

Andrew Cruickshank—"Oh! that's very true—to be revealed like this is amazing."

Michael Codron—"Yes perfectly true."

Perry Como—"Dead Right."

Ronnie Corbett—"This Fraser White goes into everything. What a remarkable accurate analysis."

Wendy Craig—"I am amazed how he can read all this from my handwriting—it is all very true."

Michael Crawford—"True—absolutely."

Peter Cushing—"It's quite, quite, quite extraordinary."

Paul Daneham—"He's absolutely right."

Michael Dennison—"Yes that is quite true."

David Dimbleby—"Oh yes that's true—a revealing analysis."

157

Val Doonican—"I think it's marvellous and absolutely fascinating."

Diana Dors—"That's true."

Michele Dotrice—"Yes that is very true. Thank you very much Fraser."

Dick Emery—"He's marvellous."

Gerald Flood—"No, but mainly yes!"

John Finch—"I cannot disagree with anything you have said about me."

Bruce Forsyth—"He's absolutely marvellous. I really mean that, he has hit on a lot of things."

Barry Foster—"Great, Fraser it's so true."

Patrick Cargill—"That's very true, it's quite amazing."

Dolores Gray—"That is a remarkable picture of myself, everything he has said is right."

Joel Grey—"True, so true."

Kenneth Haig—"Amazing absolutely true, yes."

Ty Hardin—"Dead right."

Sir Robert Helpmann—"How fascinating."

Graham Hill—"This is tremendous. I am amazed he can read all this from handwriting."

Jimmy Hill—"I must say I agree with everything. I congratulate you Fraser."

Mary Holland—"Yes, that's perfectly true."

Sally Ann Howes—"Smack-on, that's absolutely true."

Barry Humphries—"I thought it was going to be rubbish, but it was very accurate."

Gayle Hunnicut—"Bull's-eye, Fraser."

Frank Ifield—"Thst's very true."

Gordon Jackson—"Truly remarkable."

David Jacobs—"Yes he is right there."

Hattie Jacques—"Oh, yes that is so true. I am amazed."

Tom Jones—"I only hope I can live up to it."

Danny La Rue—"Boom, boom that's very true. How amazing."

Christopher Lee—"An extraordinary analysis and it's 90 per cent accurate."

Tommy Leonetti—"Incredible, it stuns me, that you can get to know a person from his handwriting."

Anna Calder Marshall—"Yes that is true, very definitely so, I am most impressed."

Virginia McKenna—"He's very good—that's true."

John Mills—"Yes that is true—yes he is right there."

Bobby Moore—"It's very, very interesting."

Patrick Moore—"That is true I agree with that, Fraser, that's very true."

Matt Monro—"Absolutely true."

Stirling Moss—"Oh, that's very good."

Pete Murray—"Absolutely right Fraser. You just wait, my lad!"

Rod McKuen—"Dead right, but why am I doing this ? Why am I bearing my soul in front of the public like this ?"

David Niven—"That's so true, I hardly dare say how much I admire your art."

Des O'Connor—"Fraser White's done a very good job. I would say he is 95 per cent accurate."

Jon Pertwee—"This man is a genius."

Leslie Phillips—"Yes very true, absolutely true I'm amazed."

Pat Phoenix—"Yes, that's true, he's right there."

Marjorie Proops—"It's a very good character reading."

Margaret Powell—"Well I am amazed."

Raymonde (Teasie Weasie)—"Quite true."

Ralph Reader—"Full marks, that's remarkable."

Beryl Reid—"I agree with that wholeheartedly, yes all that's true."

Rev Fred Secombe—"Yes that's right."

Harry Secombe—"I'm going red here!"

Peter Sellers—"Your analysis of me is quite astonishing, probably the most accurate character reading I have ever had."

Bill Simpson—"Yes, that's very true—well done Fraser."

Jacqueline Susanne—"Very interesting analysis."

Eric Sykes—"That's true, golly that's true. Well it's amazing. I am very impressed."

Jimmy Tarbuck—"Gee Fraser that's tremendous that is."

Bill Travers—"That's so right."

John Trevelyan—"Well done Fraser. That is absolutely right."

Ann Todd—"Yes that is very true."

Frankie Vaughan—"He's right there."

Norman Vaughan—"This is all frighteningly true. He's done very well on that."

Sarah Vaughan—"That's absolutely true."

Marjorie Wallace (Miss World)—"Well this is just remarkable."

Virginia Wade—"That is me alright."

Harold Wilson—"What do you mean I am not the life and soul of the party ?"

Kenneth Williams—"That is so true, a very good graphologist that bloke. My goodness he's accurate. It seems a man is known by his letter writing. Yes, he is uncanny. I think he is brilliant."

Emlyn Williams—"He is right, so right."

Nicol Williamson—"Out of all the press-cuttings on my character this is the most accurate one."

Edward Woodward—"I must say he is very good."

Jimmy Young—"I think he is very good and a lot of other people think that too."

THE END